Shaiva Devotional Songs
of Kashmir

The SUNY Series in the Shaiva Traditions of Kashmir

Harvey P. Alper, Editor

Editorial Board

Edward Dimock

Wilhem Halbfass

Gerald J. Larson

Wendy D. O'Flaherty

Andre Padoux

Navjivan Rastogi

Ludo Rocher

Alexis Sanderson

Shaiva Devotional Songs of Kashmir

●

A TRANSLATION AND
STUDY OF UTPALADEVA'S

Shivastotravali

●

Constantina Rhodes Bailly

STATE UNIVERSITY OF NEW YORK PRESS

Published by
State University of New York Press, Albany

For information, address the State University of New York Press,
90 State Street, Suite 700, Albany, NY 12207

Library of Congress Cataloging in Publication Data

Utpala, fl. 900-950.
    Shaivite devotional songs of Kashmir.

    (SUNY series in Kashmir Shaivism)
    Translation of: Śivastotrāvalī.
    Bibliography.
    1. Siva (Hindu deity)—Prayer-books and devotions—
Sanskrit. 2. Siva (Hindu deity)—Prayer-books and
devotions—English. 3. Kashmir Śaivism—Prayer-books
and devotions—Sanskrit. 4. Kashmir Śaivism—Prayer-
books and devotions—English. I. Bailly, Constantina
Rhodes. II. Title. III. Series: SUNY series in
Kashmir Śaivism.
BL1218.2.U8713 1987   294.5′43   87-6488

ISBN 0-88706-492-2
ISBN 0-88706-493-0 (pbk.)

10 9 8 7 6 5 4 3 2 1

For my parents

Contents

Contents

Acknowledgements

During the process of writing this book, many people have advised and encouraged me, almost without exception reinforcing the notion that the *Śivastotrāvalī* deserves to be brought to light in the English-speaking world.

I am deeply indebted to Ram Karan Sharma, eminent scholar and devout Śaiva, who spent many hours reviewing my translations and imparting exceptional insights based not only on his exceptional fluency in Sanskrit but through his true spirit of devotion. Both in Delhi and, after a long hiatus, in New York, the Sharmas welcomed me into their home with much warmth. I am grateful to Harvey Alper for inspiring the final vision of this book. He has offered not only sound logistic advice but an abundance of enthusiasm and kind encouragement.

During the Fifth World Sanskrit Conference in Banaras (1981) both Navjivan Rastogi and B. N. Pandit offered practical suggestions on the content of the introductory sections and on the English form of the verse translations. I thank Lilian Silburn who, though quite ill, took the time to write me letters of valuable advice and direction. André Padoux has opened my mind to the vast possibilities in the study of this literature. I thank him for enlivening conversations in Banaras, in Philadelphia, and, most importantly, in Paris, where he gave me the inspiration to take the dissertation off the shelf and proceed with turning it into a book.

For financial support I am grateful to the Department of Middle East Languages and Cultures of Columbia University, New York, for granting me the Jackson Fellowship for Sanskrit and Iranian Studies during my years in India. I am also indebted to the American Institute of Indian Studies.

Acknowledgements

For allowing me access to the Sanskrit manuscripts I am grateful to Dr. B. K. Shastri of the Sri Ranbir Sanskrit Research Library of the Raghunath Mandir, Jammu, who, along with his assistants, specially opened the library during a holiday and spent many hours with me reviewing their collection of *Śivastotrāvalī* manuscripts. In Jammu I am also indebted for their suggestions to Kaushalya Valli and Ved Kumari Ghai of the Philosophy Department of Jammu University. At the Banaras Hindu University Library I am grateful to Hari Deo Sharma. At the manuscript library of the University of Kashmir in Srinagar I am thankful to B. K. Deambi for going through the entire collection of *Śivastotrāvalī* manuscripts with me. Special heartfelt thanks are due to Pandit Dina Nath Shastri Yach of the University of Kashmir, who not only spent many hours reviewing the manuscripts with me and helped to photograph them, but who chanted large sections of the *Śivastotrāvalī* for me to record; he also brought me to receive the *darśana* of Swami Laksman Joo.

In New York, I owe much to Alex Wayman, who first opened my eyes to Sanskrit devotional hymns and who has provided years of encouragement and support. To Barbara Stoler Miller I owe my love of Sanskrit poetry; her instincts and suggestions about the form that this book might take have proven valuable. I am grateful to Kathleen R. F. Burrill, who has been a constant source of support and good faith, and a model for emulation.

Most of all I am indebted to my husband, Gene, who has showered me with endless support, invaluable spiritual insight, and unwavering faith throughout the many manifestations of this project. I thank Ophelia for her undaunted patience, and I thank Marie-Alexandra, through whom I have come to experience the intoxicating depths of *vātsalyarasa*.

Constantina Rhodes Bailly

Woodridge, New York

Introduction

Utpaladeva (*ca.* A.D. 900-950), well known as a founder of the Pratyabhijñā school of philosophy[1] in Kashmir, is best remembered for his philosophical treatises, most notably the *Īśvarapratyabhijñākārikā*, which, with its commentary, *Vimarśinī*, of Abhinavagupta, constitutes a major contribution to Indian philosophy in general. But Utpaladeva was, foremost, a highly realized devotee of Śiva, and is considered in Kashmiri tradition to have been a *siddha* ("perfected being"). The recitation of the *stotra*s, or songs, of the *Śivastotrāvalī* features in the worship of the Śaiva community of Kashmir, even to this day. Since the time of their composition they have been chanted in the same style, and it has only been in the last fifty years that a more modern, though still beautiful, style has been adopted.

The *Śivastotrāvalī* survives with the commentary of Kṣemarāja, who notes that these songs were not composed by Utpaladeva as a single, structured work, but rather were written sporadically, during particular moods of devotional joy, anguish, praise, or of the mere reflection of his own philosophical ideas. After Utpala's death, his disciples Śrīrāma and Ādityarāja are said to have been responsible for collecting the songs, which another disciple, Viśvāvartta, then divided into twenty chapters and provided with individual titles.

It is in the *stotra*s of the *Śivastotrāvalī* that the material of Utpaladeva's treatises is experienced firsthand by their author. This is not, of course, to say that a philosopher does not "experience" his material on some—usually intellectual—level. But it is in these songs that we are provided as though through a spiritual diary, the ups and downs of one who not only speculates about the path toward realization, but has tread it himself. Following him through the journey, indeed, from the very beginning, we have the sense that we are accompanying Utpala on the wanderings on a marvelous pilgrimage.

The pilgrimage, of course, is through his own interior landscape, testimony to the cosmic truth that he repeatedly strives to retain as a constant realization: that his own body is united with the body of Śiva, that is, the whole world. In his journeys we experience the wilderness that is both frightening and awe-inspiring, that makes the poet wonder desperately whether his is just a voice crying out in the vast darkness. The geography of Utpaladeva's interior pilgrimage, not surprisingly, resembles the land of Kashmir, with mountains and forests, and quite prominently, lakes with water lotuses. Along the dusty journey the wanderer seeks deep peace of mind, likened to the cool depths of a mountain lake or to a hidden mountain recess.

We may regard the opening verse of the *Śivastotrāvalī* as a benediction at the outset of the journey. A standardized obeisance to the deity or a supplication for protection might be expected before the actual subject of the piece begins. Observe, however, the object of homage in this first verse:

> We praise the one who is filled with devotion,
> Who meditates not nor recites by the rule,
> And yet without any effort at all
> Attains the splendor of Śiva. (1.1)

It is as though the opening is the very *śaktipāta* of the piece: an initial, shocking understanding is put to us, that is, to honor the devotee foremost, for the true devotee has identified completely with Śiva. This is a state that has come through the grace of Śiva and through the devotion of the individual, and therefore, in the highest realization it is indeed a eulogy of Śiva as well as the path itself, the supreme path, according to Utpaladeva, of devotion.

By setting the focus as such from the opening verse, Utpala reflects that already has he acquired insight into the reality of Śiva-consciousness. But an inkling of that vision is just beginning, and the songs of the entire *Śivastotrāvalī* are testimony to the joyful as well as painful realities of spiritual progression in an individual's life. Similarly is the pilgrim compelled by his awakened spirituality to set forth and find more.

Background of the Sanskrit Text

This book began as a doctoral dissertation[2] that presented a translation of a selection of the songs and constituted an in-depth inquiry into the status of the manuscripts and the preservation of the textual tradition of the *Śivastotrāvalī*. Between 1981 and 1983 I closely examined seven manuscripts, two in *devanāgarī* and the other five in *śāradā*, the script traditionally used in Kashmir for writing in Sanskrit. I collected the manuscripts from as wide a geographical range as possible, although, understandably, the greatest concentration of these manuscripts was to be found in Kashmir itself. (The manuscript library in the University of Kashmir, Srinagar, contains a total of thirty-four.) After careful examination I concluded that there were no major variants in any of the manuscripts that I studied, and that the textual tradition of the *Śivastotrāvalī* remained intact, without varying recensions.

The Sanskrit text of the *Śivastotrāvalī* was first published in 1902 in the Chowkhamba Sanskrit Series, and was reissued in 1964, edited by the late Swami Laksman Joo of Srinagar.[3] I did encounter some differences among the available texts—the seven manuscripts plus the 1964 published edition, which was based upon "five or six" unidentified manuscripts—but these were for the most part simply errors in *saṃdhi* or the use of synonymous terms that fit into the meter exactly, and that for the most part did not detract from the message of the verse.[4] For this book, therefore, I have followed the text as printed by the Chowkhamba Sanskrit Series.

THE PILGRIM SETS FORTH

Selecting a Path

The system put forth by Utpaladeva is essentially a religion of the householder. Thus can the spiritual quest be seen to be modeled on the activities of the pilgrim—a householder who has taken a spiritual leave of absence from worldly functions—rather than an ascetic, who has severed with them altogether.

As a heuristic device to categorize the range of experience expressed in these songs, it is useful to look at the broad categories representative of the *upāya*s ("ways, means, expedients, paths") of spiritual progress. There are three actual *upāya*s, plus a fourth, transcendent one; they can be thought of as a psychological ranking of an individual's present spiritual inclinations and his potentials. Kashmir Śaivism is often praised[5] for this psychological perceptiveness of the realities of just how each person can go about his spiritual progress and meet with neither too much challenge nor too much boredom.

The theory of the *upāya*s carries an inherent acknowledgement that the community of those following the path is comprised of a wide array of individuals; one must not wait an unknown number of lifetimes to be born into a high caste or as a male in order to worship Śiva or even dream of attaining his immediate realization; rather, the way is open not only to the high castes but also to low and even outcastes; not only to men but to women and indeed to children; not only to the renunciants but to the householder:

> Hundreds indeed are those, O Lord,
> Who through your inspiration
> While living the lives of average people
> Perceive just through these very eyes
> Your form ever before them. (12.21)

Just the mere thought—even a negative one—is enough to set the process into motion:

> Even for him whose thought of worshiping you
> Arises only hypocritically,
> Inevitably he acquires an appropriate
> Closeness to you. (12.10)

That the way is open to all creatures is another way of acknowledging the conviction that with the body of Śiva as the whole universe and all in it, what or who indeed is not the same as the worshiper himself?

What, then, are the different *upāya*s? The first, *āṇava upāya* ("the path of minuteness") is for those individuals most subject to *āṇava*, or minuteness, and whose consciousness has therefore become highly limited or bound. In this *upāya* much emphasis is placed on personal effort, focused particularly on the realm of the senses. Thus ritual (i.e., the sights and smells of flowers, bells, incense, abstract and concrete images, statues, etc.), repetition of *mantra*s (for control of the mind), and *prāṇāyāma* (for control of the breath and the subtle channels called *nāḍī*s) are prescribed.

The second, *śākta upāya* ("the way of power"), or *jñāna upāya* ("the way of knowledge") places a greater emphasis on mental awareness. The practitioner's sense of duality begins to fade, but he is still fixed with a dualist vision; for this reason this way is also called *bhedābheda upāya* ("the way of difference and nondifference").

The third *upāya* is *śāmbhava upāya* ("the way of Śambhu or Śiva"). It entails a highly evolved consciousness whereby the will (*icchā*) predominates; it is thus also called *icchā upāya* ("the way of the will"). In this *upāya* the practitioner can induce at will and retain for long periods a fixed awareness of the universe as pure consciousness.

The fourth and highest *upāya*, like the fourth constituent of other Indian mystical progressions, is not a true *upāya* as such but represents the transcendence of the *upāya*s themselves. Thus it is called *anupāya* ("wayless, without a way"), or *ānanda upāya* ("the way of bliss"). It requires almost no spiritual discipline, for the practitioner has entered into a state of absolute realization, where, as we saw in the opening verse of the *Śivastotrāvalī*, the practitioner is beyond the need for meditation or the counting of prayer beads. Thus it is also known as *pratyabhijñā upāya* ("the way of recognition").

Using the categories of the *upāya*s facilitates encompassing the broad range of experiences of one on the path. More than anything, the *upāya*s are categories of psychological tendency, each of which is expressed throughout the *Śivastotrāvalī*. Unlike a philosophical treatise, it does not guide the reader through a steady progression, as, for example, the *Yogasūtra* of Patañjali, which delineates the stages of yoga from "lowest" to "highest." The *Śivastotrāvalī*, rather, takes the reader along the winding path of discovery. In several places Utpala calls this path of devotion a creeper, that is, a vine that haltingly makes its way but that bears marvelous fruits.

Introduction

In the Realm of the Senses

Beginning with the realm of the senses, we can now take a longer look at the imagery of the sensual world as it appears in these songs. We have already considered the image of the pilgrim roaming about in the world of Śiva. Every place, indeed, becomes a sacred *tīrtha*, a ford for crossing over into Śiva's realm. Thus, in the midst of the ordinary world, one need only to shift perspective—a shift toward Śiva-consciousness—to experience the difference; such a difference is possible for the true devotee:

> Even the path of worldly living
> Becomes blissful for the devotees
> Who have obtained your blessing, O Lord,
> And who live inside your realm. (1.3)

Thus it is along the journey through the ordinary world, by means of the faculties of sense, that the devotee searches for a vision of Śiva-consciousness. But like the journeyer through the wilderness fearful of dacoits, Utpala recognizes the threat of ever-lurking "sense-thieves" along the way:

> O Celestial One, grant that I may overcome
> The enemies along your path,
> The sense-thieves
> Who conceal the highest reality. (19.11)

Indeed, the sensual world consists of Citi, divine consciousness as the body of Śakti; the senses and the physical body that confine one to bondage also constitute the vehicle for liberation. Thus the well-known tantric adage: "The very poison that kills becomes the elixir of life when used by the wise."[6] It is for this reason that not only are the senses acknowledged, but they are to be strengthened:

> Nourished by the nectar
> Of pure devotion rippling within,
> Let my body become fit for your worship. (17.26)

It is for two reasons that the senses are to be strengthened: first, so that

6

they be a strong vehicle for the descent of the power of Śiva, which constitutes not just a feeling of emotional wellbeing, but a true force of the power of nature; *śaktipāta* is the descent of *śakti*, or power, of Śiva in the form of the natural world. This *śakti* is akin to lightning, electricity, and ultimately the atomic energy that Śiva "dances up" in the dissolution of the universe. Second, by becoming a vessel for divine power, the practitioner is also emulating nature itself, just a step away from the body of Śiva, made of pure consciousness. Embodied by Śakti, nature is also then a vessel; Utpala refers to Devī as the "treasury of all powers" (14.13).

But if the senses are to be strengthened, they are to be dedicated to Śiva: giving up one's senses is but loosing them, and thus the devotee beseeches:

While incessantly drinking in through the senses
The heady wine of your worship
From the overflowing goblets of all objects,
Let madness overtake me. (13.8)

The field of worship, then, is the individual himself. The turning inward to perform the sacrifice is similar to the concept in the Upaniṣads whereby the external elements of Vedic sacrifice—the animals, plants, and special locale—were redesignated to interior ones, in the human body and psyche. But whereas the Upaniṣads had the practice retreat from society, the Pratyabhijñā Śāstra brings it back: thus worship, though not *of* the world, flourishes in its very midst.

Pratyabhijñā Śāstra speaks of the five *kañcuka*s, or coverings of *māyā*, that is, the limitations on the individual consciousness. They are a false sense in regard to *rāga* (enjoyment), *kāla* (time or mortality), *niyati* (pervasiveness of space), *vidyā* (knowledge), and *kalā* (authorship).

Rāga relates directly to man as a *paśu*, a "beast" tethered by his deepest uncontrollable desires, attachments, and illusions. One must seek to overcome the limitation of *rāga* by redirecting it and putting it to one's use toward furthering an understanding of his true nature. Gaining control over the false sense of enjoyment in this way, the devotee ultimately learns to live fully within the world of *saṃsāra* while remaining unattached to it. The devotee understands that the task of redirecting *rāga* and the other limitations is beyond his own means; he recognizes that the *kañcuka*s are manifestations of Śiva and that Śiva has ultimate mastery over them.

Introduction

Thus he offers them in sacrifice to the Lord:

> Accept false enjoyment and the other limitations
> That I offer unto you, O Lord.
> Having transformed them into immortal nectar,
> Enjoy them together with the devotees. (5.13)

By giving up worldly enjoyment one does not give up pleasures; he discovers instead a different source of delight, the joy that emanates from becoming centered in the identification of one's true self. The farther one comes from the bondage of his false viewpoint, the deeper becomes his enjoyment of unification with the Lord.

Rāga has a wide range of related interpretations; it indicates color, redness, inflammation, and thus passion, enjoyment, attachment, delight, and love. In certain respects, *rāga* as such is not a hindrance to liberation, but rather qualifies an instrument towards it. As joy, delight, love, and even attachment, *rāga* is a quality not to be extinguished but understood and nourished appropriately:

> O Lord, enlighten my heart!
> Help me to discriminate between
> The base delight in false enjoyments
> And the superior delight in your lotus feet. (5.20)

As a color, *rāga* is seen as a stain that, when offered to Śiva, becomes lost in and purified by the white brilliance of the god's impeccable splendor.

The Pratyabhijñā Śāstra recognizes five *indriyas*, or faculties of sense: *rasa* (taste), *ghrāṇa* (smell), *darśana* (sight), *śravaṇa* (hearing), and *sparśa* (touch). In the process of merging with the Lord, the devotee requests that in addition to *rāga*, the *indriyas* also maintain their worldly functions, but that they no longer create a hindrance to true recognition of the self. Rather, says Utpala:

> Let the sense faculties, full of delight,
> Be attached to their respective objects.
> But may there not be, even for an instant,
> Any loss of the joy
> Of your nonduality. (8.5)

The joy of such a vision is not readily attained, however, when the senses remain stubbornly immersed in self-consciousness. Without the energy of Śakti to operate them, the faculties of sense cannot function. But the individual self persists, through its pride, in reverting to the attitude that the senses belong to, and operate for the benefit of, the limited self alone:

> Enlivened by you, these senses quiver
> Though they be like lumps of clay.
> They dance, like feathery fluffs of cotton
> Raised up by the breeze.
>
> If, O Lord, the senses were not
> Endowed with self-consciousness,
> Then who would forsake the realization
> That the world is one with you? (10.18,19)

Each of the senses receives separate attention in the *Śivastotrāvalī*, but the sense of taste (*rasa*) has special significance, particularly as regards what Utpala points out as *rasa* in varying situations. *Rasa* is one of those Sanskrit words that almost defies translation by virtue of its rich and varied multiplicity of equivalent words in English. In one respect, *rasa* means *sentiment*; what is called the "*rasa* of devotion" in these poems denotes a sentiment felt by the devotee toward the object of devotion. *Rasa* also means *taste, flavor*, or *savor*, and thus the "*rasa* of devotion" in this respect indicates a pleasurable sensory experience—indeed, a taste— that is an outcome of devotion. Thus as sentiment, *rasa* is that which the devotee "puts into" his act of worship; as flavor, it is that which he receives, or "gets out" of it. Thirdly, *rasa* is syrup, sap, pith, resin, or nectar, and Utpala makes frequent use of the image of *rasa* as the extract of a plant. When in a state of mystic union, the aspirant is said to taste a sweet and intoxicating nectar, sometimes called *amṛta* and at other times called *rasa*. Finally, Pratyabhijñā has a special connotation for the term: the essential "stuff" of Paramaśiva from which Śiva and Śakti become manifest is known as *śivarasa*.

The connotations of sentiment, savor, juice, pith, and the core essence of Śiva all are called to mind with the term as Utpala uses it—as he does often—in the *Stotrāvalī*. In some instances I have chosen to translate *rasa* as somewhere between *sentiment* (as effusive emotion), *pith* (as extract),

9

and *nectar* (as sweet or intoxicating) with the English word *spirit.*

Just as he learns to redirect and thus reintegrate his sensory faculties, the aspirant learns that he must perceive the forms within the world of *saṃsāra* as manifestations of the body of Śiva. That the universe is inlaid with the form of Śiva is further expressed with the concept of that form as a city; the body of Śiva consists of a pattern, a map with the paths and subtle currents (*nāḍīs,* meaning the veins, arteries, and pulses of the physical and subtle bodies, into which we may read the geographical connection with rivers) along which the devotee travels in meditation. This is a type of *maṇḍala,* or mystic diagram representing both the universe without and the universe that exists within the individual. Utpaladeva indicates that by treading the path within the city of Śiva, the devotee can change in a positive way his movements along the path through the world of *saṃsāra.* Thus the devotee sometimes expresses his wish for union as dwelling inside of the Lord, and at other times, he depicts this specifically as dwelling inside the city of Śiva.

While in the state of perceiving the difference between subject and object, the devotee remains outside of the city of Śiva; the city is a *pur,* that is, a town or fortress enclosed by a wall in every direction, and accessible only by a huge, reinforced gate. As such the *pur* of Śiva is also the body of the individual *puruṣa.* Within, it contains eight *cakras,* and as entrance-ways, it has nine orifices, or "city gates."[7]

Even the aspirant who approaches with utmost devotion encounters difficulty in gaining access to the innermost heart of that city:

> This terrible world is about to be ended.
> The deep stain of my mind has melted away.
> Still the gates of your city
> Are bolted shut
> And do not unlatch even slightly. (4.15)

Even though the devotee may overcome the "stains" of the memory of the false attachment to worldly objects, the gates to the center of the city do not easily open. But since the city is located within the individual himself, Utpaladeva is saying here that the aspirant's devotion is not yet strong enough to break the latches, for if the gates circumscribe Śiva's city, they define the boundaries of the human heart as well. The "unlatching," then, is also the piercing of the heart *cakra* (*anāhatacakra*), and either action requires both the will of Śiva and the incentive of the individual. Thus the devotee asks the Lord not only to bestow grace, but to help deepen his own devotion:

> When shall my mind
> Indifferent to all else through love's intensity
> Tear open the great door latch
> With a loud bang
> And finally arrive in your presence, O Lord? (9.3)

A related image is that of the royal chamber, and with this Utpaladeva shows that even the supreme Vedic gods are denied access to the inner heart of Śiva. Here, Viṣṇu, Indra, and Brahmā cannot be admitted because they are not devotees; this reflects also Utpala's view of the inadequacy of Vedic worship in which ritual overrides devotion:

> Forever may I sing my praises
> Loudly to you,
> Located in that place where Hari,
> Haryaśva, and Viriñca are waiting outside. (7.7)

The only deity to dwell there is Devī, one of the many personifications of Śakti. Śakti is the primal energy of the universe, and Śiva is the universal consciousness; as such they are two complementary aspects of the universal Paramaśiva, seemingly separate but constantly united. When personified as deities, Śiva and Śakti are recognized as being eternally united through mutual devotion; they dwell always in the same place:

> May I live in that sanctuary, O Lord,
> Where, taking many forms,
> You reside with Devī
> From the palace up to the city gates. (5.7)

Just as the latched gates of the city of Śiva are a tantric image representing the as yet unliberated state of the aspirant, so also is the image of the knot with which the soul has been bound. Utpaladeva speaks of the knot that fastens the devotee into bondage; the knot keeps the devotee from realizing his true nature, and as such is a form of illusion. But the

11

efficacy of that illusion is all the more powerful because it, too, is an aspect of Śiva. Utpala reiterates that liberation must be sought by the very force that causes bondage:

> Alas, O Lord, this knot of the soul
> Prevents your realization.
> But fashioned and concealed by you,
> That knot is strong indeed—
> So strong that, disregarding you,
> It slackens not a bit. (4.24)

Thus the devotee understands, intellectually, the source of his feeling of separation from the Lord. He understands also that to transform his false viewpoint of self-identification, he must perceive enjoyment, the faculties of sense, the individual body, and indeed the form of the whole world as manifestations of Śiva and thus of himself. He thus petitions:

> In speech, in thought,
> In the perceptions of the mind,
> And in the gestures of the body,
> May the sentiment of devotion be my companion
> At all times, in all places. (5.22)

The experience of merging with Śiva is often described in these songs as sweetened with *amṛta*, or celestial nectar, and the path of the devotee is said repeatedly to be sweetened with the "nectar of devotion." This nectar is also an intoxicating wine, as, for example:

> With my eyes closed
> At the touch of your lotus feet,
> May I rejoice,
> Reeling with drunkenness
> From the wine of your devotion. (5.5)

By offering up the restrictive, worldly-bound senses, the devotee takes leave of them: this is the joy of delightful worship. And that intoxication, according to Utpala, will never be experienced by one treading on any other path, even the revered path of *jñāna* (intellectual knowledge). On the contrary:

The highest state of intellectual knowledge
Has none of the taste of the nectar
Of your devotion.
To me, O Lord, it is like sour wine. (1.11)

In some of the songs the sense of sight is interpreted literally. Yearning for a vision, which in a higher sense indicates spiritual realization, also takes the form of an ecstatic vision, as a visitation of the beloved deity:

Ardently I desire to behold
Your ever-blossoming lotus face.
O Lord, may you appear to me,
Howsoever faintly,
Face to face. (4.16)

The *Śivastotrāvalī* is filled with expressions of how the devotee seeks to redirect these senses as well as those of touch, smell, and hearing toward the wholistic experience of Śiva-consciousness.

MANY PATHS, ONE PATH

At a certain point the aspirant begins to take hold more securely in his practice. These positive gains are spoken of in terms of undoing, of dissolution: he begins to *lose* his sense of duality, he *unties* the knots that bind him, he *breaks open* the latch to the gate of the city that is Śiva. These things begin to happen, that is, his awareness of his true identity begins to become more apparent, by means of his perseverance to the task, which, in this system, comes down to the faith and devotion (*bhakti*) that he cultivates in his heart.

This stage, which we may equate with the level of *śākta upāya* ("the way of power"), or *jñāna upāya* ("the way of knowledge"), entails the development of both power and knowledge: *śakti* is power, that is, the constrictive power of the natural world, as well as the power to overcome that world. Knowledge involves a higher intellectual understanding of the spiritual endeavor.

The powers developed by the aspirant are called *siddhi*s

Introduction

("perfections"). The *siddhi*s are powers to manipulate and transcend nature and the natural world; they are, then, supernatural powers. They consist of *śakti* (the manifestation of nature, the first evolute, personified as Śakti); thus to acquire them means to identify with Śakti herself, and consequently with Śiva-consciousness.

The natural world, or Śakti, is also called *māyā* (personified as Māyā), from which derives the English word *magic*. The *siddhi*s are "magical" powers in both ways in which magic is understood: They are sleight of hand, the art of illusion, and they are, as perhaps the most distinctive feature of primal religions, manipulation of the elements of nature.

The acquisition and accumulation of these powers is recognized as a byproduct of many spiritual paths. As in Patañjali's *Yogasūtra*, for example, Pratyabhijñā stresses the necessity for the ethical cultivation of these powers. Undue attachment to an accumulation of *siddhi*s detracts from the ultimate goal of the *siddhi*s, liberation itself. And misguided attachments to the *siddhi*s, that is, using them for malicious purposes, degenerates into black magic.

Referred to collectively, they are known as *aṣṭasiddhi*, or the "eight perfections"; Utpaladeva refers to them as *aṇimādi*, or "*aṇimā* and the other [powers]." They are, in their traditional order, the faculty or ability to acquire (1) *aṇimā* (infinitely small size); (2) *mahimā* (infinitely large size); (3) *laghimā* (infinitely light weight); (4) *garimā* (infinite heaviness); (5) *prāpti* (transporting oneself by mere thought); (6) *prākāmya* (having everything in plenty); (7) *īśitva* (overlordship, domination); and (8) *vaśitva* (ability to subjugate anyone or anything).

The *siddhi*s exist so that the aspirant can strengthen himself in his spiritual pursuit: that pursuit, then, is also an adventure into the higher realms of the natural world; awareness becomes strengthened and nourished as one crosses into this realm that exists at the fringes of completely worldly consciousness at one extreme and at the other, the absolute consciousness of Śiva. This is a crossing place, a ford, indeed, the very definition of a twilight zone. Here one goes back and forth between a consciousness fixed in duality and nonduality; thus it is called *bhedābheda*.

Grace and Devotion

It is said that the heart's spiritual yearnings are brought about either by an innate desire or by some shocking experience or realization. In several places Utpaladeva attributes his treading the spiritual path to Śiva—sometimes rejoicing in the fact, and sometimes lamenting it.

The process of how the *siddhi*s come about serves as a paradigm for the very process of spiritual evolution itself. In introducing the concept, I use the term "come about" in a purposeful avoidance, for the moment, of either the phrase "how the aspirant develops his powers" or "how the powers are acquired." For inherent in such language would have been the implied agent of action, and this points to the very crux of the question, not only as regards the evolution of the *siddhi*s, but of liberation itself. How does one set foot on the path? How does one reach its highest goal? Here we encounter the enigma that lies at the core of the *Śivastotrāvalī*—the ambiguous relationship between *anugraha* ("grace") and *bhakti* ("devotion").

If we take a second look at that "dissolution" terminology of the spiritually progressing aspirant, we will see that in some places he is said to lose his sense of duality, in others, that the duality *is removed*; here he unties the knots, elsewhere they *are untied*; sometimes he must break open the latch, at others, the door *swings open* for him.

On an even more subtle level, Utpaladeva expresses this brilliantly with his use of the term *tvadbhakti*, perhaps, along with *tvadbhaktirasa*, the most frequently occurring phrase in the *Śivastotrāvalī*. The simplest way to render *tvadbhakti* into English is, literally, "your devotion," a phrase that carries the original ambiguity: it denotes both "*x*'s devotion to you" and "your devotion to *x*." In just one of many examples, Utpala implores:

> Just as Devī,
> Your most beloved, endless pool of bliss,
> Is inseparable from you,
> So may your devotion alone
> Be inseparable from me. (1.9)

For Utpaladeva the path of devotion is the most supreme and efficacious form of worship; thus he asks that his devotion to the Lord be a strong, integral part of himself. But equally apparent—by its intentional ambiguity—is the prayer that the Lord, in the same way that he sheds devotion upon Devī, shed devotion on the devotee. Perhaps at the heart of this ambiguity lies the very concept of *bhakti* itself: literally a "share" or "allotment," its original meaning focuses on the apportionment itself, not on who does the apportioning.

Utpala has another term for the other side of this process, however: *anugraha*, or grace. It is Utpala's conviction that one cannot even experience devotion without an initial stroke of grace. The two—devotion and grace—operate together as two aspects of the same entity, ultimately showing their common goal, or, from a different viewpoint, their common source. Through a dualistic consciousness, the two are separate processes: in one, the devotee (as subject) extends the feeling of devotion toward the Lord (as object); in the other, the Lord (as subject) bestows grace upon the devotee (as object). The dualistic process is a means to achieve the realization that the two are united in their common goal as well as in their common source, the body of Śiva:

> When will that small amount of grace
> Abiding with the Lord
> And that small amount of devotion
> That has come to me
> Unite to become like that unique form—
> The blissful body of Śiva? (8.1)

Utpala is the first to admit, however, that the true relationship between grace and devotion remains a mystery:

> You are pleased, O Lord, with devotion,
> And devotion arises at your will.
> You alone understand
> How these are connected. (16.21)

In the state of absolute realization one perceives the process of devotion and grace as two aspects of one divine process. The sense of duality that is perceived is the same that is produced when the universe is manifested as the complementary aspects of Śiva and Śakti, typified in turn by the complementary qualities of the manifest universe, *prakāśa* and *vimarśa*: *Prakāśa* is illumination, the placid, transcendent Śiva. *Vimarśa* is the dynamic, immanent Śakti; they may be considered, in Arabinda Basu's words, the "background" and "foreground," respectively.[8] Beyond the personifications of Śiva and Śakti lie the cosmological images of

16

prakāśa and *vimarśa*. Harvey P. Alper points out just two of the images evoked by *prakāśa*:

> ... *prakāśa* as spacial effervescence, and *prakāśa* as the sea at the heart of all things. . . . The theology of *prakāśa* hints at the dissolution of ordinary ego consciousness, at immersion in the cave, the bottomless center of all phenomena; it seems to speak of overflowing, being brimful, of being afloat in the depths of the sea.[9]

Before going on to observe the further importance of *prakāśa* and *vimarśa* in light of the *Śivastotrāvalī*, it is necessary here to mention the phenomenon in Pratyabhijñā known as *spanda*. *Spanda* is the initial vibration of the universe, its very heartbeat. In the *Śivadṛṣṭi* Somānanda explains *spanda*:

> This tension is perceptible in the locus of the heart when one remembers suddenly a thing that must be done at the moment, when one receives good news, when one experiences fear unexpectedly, when he sees a dear one whom he had not seen for a long time, when one pronounces emission, when one reads quickly, when one runs fast, etc. On each of these occasions there is a mingling of all the powers (*sarvaśakti vilolatā*).[10]

This "mingling of all the powers" is a characteristic of practice on the path of *śākta upāya*; thus the aspirant begins to get to the very essence of the cosmic vibration, that is, consciousness itself.

The key to the whole process—the initial vibration (*spanda*) that drums up, as it were, the two opposing entities of *prakāśa* and *vimarśa*, and, in turn, how these universal principles relate on the individual level as grace and devotion—is presented in the *Anubhāva Sūtra*:

> Śiva's innate power Spanda is wholly responsible for the entire creation of the Universe and the same power reacting in the individual leading to final liberation is called Bhakti (devotion). The same power, Spanda, in the reverse trend is liberation. *In reality there is no difference between Śakti and Bhakti—the operating forces of Spanda.* [Italics mine][11]

Thus grace may be seen as a manifestation of *prakāśa*, emanating from the

Introduction

world as Śiva, transcendent, constant, and eternal. Devotion, in turn, is *vimarśa*; it is the sense of "I" or the individual expression through infinite variations. Devotion is dynamic, ever-seeking, ever-changing, while at the same time complemented by the steady illumination that is grace.

The philosophy of Pratyabhijñā considers *anugraha* as the only one of the five eternal processes of Śiva that is absolutely necessary for the liberation of the individual self. Thus in the *Śivastotrāvalī* Utpaladeva focuses on grace and on its complementary aspect, manifest in the individual as devotion. At times he beseeches the Lord for grace; at others, where we might expect to find him asking for grace, the prayer instead is for a strengthening of devotion:

> When shall my yearning for devotion—
> The highest state of knowledge and
> The highest state of yoga—
> Become fulfilled, O Lord? (9.9)

"Tremblings along the Journey"

We have explored, then, what the Pratyabhijñā philosophers would tell us about grace and devotion, *prakāśa* and *vimarśa*, the personifications of Śiva and Śakti, and the divine, eternal vibration that is *spanda*. How does all of this fit into the experiences of our spiritual seeker continuing his way on his pilgrimage?

At this point he has developed enough of an awareness to have gotten an inkling into his true identity, but has not acquired the spiritual acumen to increase these glimpses at will. These albeit brief experiences of his true nature provide such a contrast to his mundane vision that the acknowledgement of the difference between the states causes great spiritual anguish. He understands that although he seeks liberation from the state of dualistic perception, he constantly loses his way:

> There is no other happiness here in this world
> Than to be free of the thought
> That I am different from you.
> What other happiness is there?
> How is it, then, that still this devotee of yours
> Treads the wrong path? (4.17)

The sixth song, entitled "Tremblings along the Journey," laments repeatedly the anguish caused by the unsteadiness of this vision; the splendor of the vision makes it all the more difficult to live without:

From the center of the world
Let there be visible to me
Your magnificent jewel
That dispels the depths of darkness
With its radiant luster.

On what site do you not dwell?
What exists that does not exist in your body?
I am wearied!
Therefore let me reach you everywhere,
Without difficulty. (6.8, 9)

A devotee anxiously awaiting recognition is the image depicted in the entire ninth song; each verse contains the plaintive cry, "When shall . . . ?" It is with such plaintiveness that the songs take on the tone of an intimate relationship, with the Lord as the elusive lover, a motif known to Tamil *bhakti* poetry and that would several centuries later sweep across northern India with the great *bhakti* poets of the middle ages. Here Utpaladeva addresses the Lord as the beloved, cornering him, finally, and disrobing him—of his veil of *māyā*:

When shall that moment come, O Lord,
When all of a sudden I recognize you,
The Fearless, Exalted, Whole, Without Cause,
The One, indeed, to have veiled himself—
And in so doing make you ashamed? (9.6)

In this stage, or realm, where all is flickering, wavering, where the Lord is sometimes depicted as an abstract object of beauty and at others personified as a lover, the mood of the devotee also ranges from high to low. The devotee has glimpsed ecstacy:

I roar! Oh, and I dance!
My heart's desires are fulfilled
Now that you, Lord,

Introduction

Infinitely splendid,
Have come to me. (3.11)

He now begs to "firmly clasp" that realization:

When shall I become helplessly enraptured
And reveal to everyone my joy,
Having suddenly obtained and firmly clasped
The treasure of your most precious feet? (9.10)

In *jñāna upāya* the individual has some, but not complete understanding:

When I touch the soles of your feet,
It sometimes flashes in my mind
That this whole world
Has merged into a lake of nectar.
Lord! Grant this to me always! (5.26)

But caught up in the world, hindered by the darkness of his own stubborn mind, Utpala laments that the realization is not yet constant, and repeatedly we encounter verses that reflect the depression and anguish of one who cannot sustain that beatific vision:

Endless is the cycle of birth and death.
These slender limbs are consumed
By diseases harsh and diverse.
I have derived no real enjoyment
From pleasures of the senses.
What happiness encountered was not long lasting.
Thus, my existence has become useless.
Grant me, O Lord,
Those sublime and everlasting treasures
So that I may become your devotee
With my head illumined by touching the feet
Of the One adorned with the moon. (15.19)

In this wavering stage the devotee is thus fraught with contradictions. In some verses he begs for *aṇimā* and the other powers; in others, he boasts that he has no use for them. Similarly, in some places he extols the benefits of meditation; in others, that, too, has no use. In several instances he separates himself, as a devotee, from the (lowlier) ordinary people of the world; other verses have him begging to lead a normal life. And although Utpaladeva ever extols the ease with which the Lord is attained through devotion (as opposed to other paths), still, time and again he laments not being able to sustain that vision.

THE HIGHEST PATH AND BEYOND

We come now to the path of *śāmbhava upāya*, the path of Śiva, also called *icchā upāya*, or the way of the will, for here, the vision of absolute identity can be induced at will. Here the world is understood as the emanation of Śiva and Śakti through play (*krīḍā*); thus everything is seen as vibrating with the delightful sensation of the cosmic pulse, *spanda*. Thus do the true devotees partake of this playfulness:

> O Lord of the Universe!
> How lucky are your devotees,
> Worthy of being adored by you.
> For them, this turbulent ocean of the world
> Is like a great pleasure-lake
> For their amusement. (3.15)

In *śāmbhava upāya* worship becomes automatic, a sweet habit "unsullied" by the mere petitions that characterize the less advanced stages. Thus Utpala praises the highly attained devotee:

> Whose consciousness is expanded
> With intense devotion
> Has a unique, praiseworthy style of worship
> Unsullied by entreaties, O Granter of Boons. (17.24)

Śiva Immanent and Transcendent

Having transcended the need for the accoutrements of worship, and thus of any path at all, the devotee enjoys *svātantrya*, the true freedom of realization; this is the fourth way, *anupāya*, the supreme condition of having no path at all. Unencumbered by worldly attachments, and having surpassed the flickerings of an unsteady mind and perceptions, the perfected worshiper surpasses the realm of lamentations. Instead, his worship becomes spontaneous praise and glorification.

The fourteenth song consists solely of glorifications, and it is no wonder that in Kashmir it is the best-loved song of the *Śivastotrāvalī*. The imagery of these glorification *stotra*s reflects that, by having transcended the vision of duality in the world, that is, by having identified with the absolute consciousness of Śiva, one is free then to come full circle—to adore Śiva in his many names and forms without the fear of becoming only attached to that singular image: for the realized devotee, Śiva is at once both immanent and transcendent.

Thus it is in these songs that we encounter some of the richest imagery in the *Śivastotrāvalī* as regards iconography and the particulars of mythological episodes. For example:

> May you be glorified, anointed with moonlight
> Reflected in the vast ocean of milk.
> May you be glorified, O Lord whose ornaments
> Are snakes dazzling with jewels
> Begotten at your touch. (14.6)

Also lauded here are the salvific powers of Śiva:

> May you be glorified,
> The only lamp for worldly beings
> Blinded by the darkness of delusion.
> May you be glorified, O Supreme Person,
> Ever awake in the midst of a sleeping world. (14.18)

In the state of highest realization, the true path of Śiva is no path at all, that is, one wanders about at will, no longer having to rely on the techniques of counting beads, of retaining the breath, or even, as we saw in the very first verse, of meditation. The special quality of devotion is that it is both the means and the end; it is the one means that is not discarded at the end of the journey, for it constitutes the journey as well as its highest goal. The process of treading the path itself entails the *becoming* of a devotee; thus is the well-known adage here reworded:

"One should worship Śiva by becoming Śiva"
Is the old saying. But the devotees say,
"One should worship Śiva by becoming a devotee."
For they can recognize your essence as nondual,
Even when it is in bodily form. (1.14)

The pilgrim roams about the whole world, with every act consecrated and every place a sacred spot, a ford between the world of limitation and the world of freedom. The true wanderer in spirit is beyond fear; he is not threatened by bonds to the senses or by the surprises of the wilderness into which he has ventured. In a cosmic sense he enters the realm of the transcendent body of Śiva-consciousness. In a "name-and-form" sense, this indicates the wild realm that belongs to Śiva: the vast, dark forests full of wild animals, where ghosts linger in craggy trees.

At the end of the *Śivastotrāvalī* Utpaladeva thus calls the truly realized beings *virajana*: the valiant, the brave, the adventurers. They are beyond the ordinary person's abhorrence of ghosts, fearsome reminders of the chilly existence between hearty life and peaceful death. The realm of ghosts could only be presided over by Śiva, who pounds the world into dissolution with the fury of his cosmic dance. Thus is he glorified:

Homage to the one wearing as raiment
His own lustrous halo of radiant beams,
Bedecked with a glittering garland of skulls
For the festival of dance at the end of the world. (20.2)

Only the true devotee of Śiva could revel in what for those bound by limitation is a horrifying prospect:

As though saturated with the wine
Of the nectar of devotion,
With vital organs radiating with delight,
The adventurous ones dance through the night
With Śiva's attendants, a party of ghosts. (20.20)

And so has the accomplished devotee become a *siddha*, having mastered, by his devotion and by divine grace, the vision of true identity, abounding in freedom and beyond all fear.

Introduction

THE PROVINCE OF SACRED POETRY

Beyond the images and ideas presented in the songs of the *Śivastotrāvalī* lies the vessel for the thoughts themselves: the literary form of the *stotra*. It has been traditionally understood that *stotra* literature is composed by those of a highly evolved spiritual as well as poetic awareness.

Indeed, we do not for a moment question the spirituality of Utpaladeva. We have seen, on the other hand, the array of poetic imagery throughout the *Śivastotrāvalī*. In addition, Utpala experimented with— and employed to a perfection—a variety of complex Sanskrit meters, both syllabic (*śloka, śikhariṇī, pṛthvī, rathoddhatā,* and *śārdūlavikrīḍita*) and moraic (*āryā* and *vaitālīya*).

The classic *stotrakāra* (literally, "hymn-maker") had the gift of insight into the divine realms and could communicate this insight through verse. Mariasusai Dhavamony says of the *stotra* literature:

There is undoubtedly an appeal to the deepening of the religious sense of man. Over and above this visible, so to say, aspect of man's communion with the Deity, there is also the invisible aspect that underlies these hymns. In order to understand and interpret this spiritual aspect, we have to enter into the secret and mystical world of these hymns, a world that is beyond the grasp of ordinary human beings but nonetheless the presence of it is felt very strongly by the hymnologists.[12]

This "secret and mystical world" represents the place or faculty by which one experiences communion with the deity; Dhavamony continues:

The Indian mind is constantly seeking hidden correspondences between the world of men and the world of the gods, as is evident in the early religious literature of India. . . .[13]

The recitation or singing of the *stotra* is beneficial for the devotee, for it is a medium through which one can both vent a spiritual longing as well as rejoice in spiritual satisfaction. The very act of participating in the *stotra*, either by listening or by joining in the recitation, induces the mood of devotion. It is when the devotional mood is aroused and sustained that one can open one's heart toward divine union, which can be known about,

24

but never experienced, through the mind.

The purpose of chanting is not only for the benefit of the devotee, but for the pleasure of the gods. Indeed, the first activity of the day in the Hindu temple is to wake up the deity by singing a devotional song before the image, and the last one at night is to sing the deity to sleep. The devotee expresses love of the deity by thus cherishing and nurturing him, and similarly, the deity, entertained by the sound of the poetry and pleased by the devotion in the heart of the worshiper, bestows on him his grace. Indeed, Śiva is said to enjoy singing and dancing in his worship:

> May you be glorified, who delight in offerings
> Drenched in the sentiment of devotion.
> May you be glorified, pleased with the singing
> And dancing of devotees drunk on your wine. (14.10)

Something there is that connects the realm of the deity and that of the worshiper, something that acts as a conduit between grace and devotion. The *Śivastotrāvalī* has been called a sacred stream that flows between this world and the world of the gods, consecrating everything along its course. Madhurāja-yogin, a disciple of Abhinavagupta (and thereby a direct preceptorial descendent of Utpaladeva) so praises the *Śivastotrāvalī*:

> Though there are over thousands of
> Streams of beautiful verses,
> None at all compares to that
> Celestial river, the *Stotrāvalī*.
> As soon as it passes through the *tīrtha* of the ear
> It purifies the soul of man,
> And flows on to the throat,
> Where lies the city of Śrīkaṇṭha.[14]

Thus in describing the inner journeys of the spiritual pilgrim, the *Śivastotrāvalī* itself is called a river that flows from one realm to the next. From without, it touches on the water-shrine (*tīrtha*) of the ear, flowing down, onwards to the city of Śrīkaṇṭha, that is, Śiva as the Lord of the Throat (that has turned blue from drinking the poison of the ills of the world): one's soul becomes purified, says the devotee, by merely hearing the verses of the *Śivastotrāvalī*.

The Śivastotrāvalī

The First Song

•

The Pleasure of Devotion

oṃ

We praise the one who is filled with devotion,   1
Who meditates not nor recites by the rule,
And yet without any effort at all
Attains the splendor of Śiva.

Though my soul is young   2
Drinking the nectar of your devotion,
It is yet as one gone grey,
With hair whitened by the dust
Along this journey through the world.

Even the path of worldly living   3
Becomes blissful for the devotees
Who have obtained your blessing, O Lord,
And who live inside your realm.

When everything in the world is in your form,   4
How could there be a place
Not suitable for devotees?
Where in the world does their *mantra*
Fail to bear fruit?*

Triumphant are they, intoxicated   5
With the celestial drink of devotion.

---

* That is, is there any place at all that is not the same as a sacred pilgrimage center
for a devotee?

They are beyond duality
Yet retain you as "the other."*

6   Only those who are immersed
In the joy of fervent devotion
Know the essence, O Lord,
Of your boundless ocean of bliss.

7   You alone, O Lord, are the self of all.
And everyone naturally loves his own self.
Thus victorious becomes the one who knows
That devotion is inherent in all.

8   Lord! When the objective world has dissolved
Through a state of deep meditation,
You stand alone—
And who does not see you then?
But even in the state of differentiation
Between the knower and the known,
You are easily seen by the devotees.†

9   Just as Devī,
Your most beloved, endless pool of bliss,
Is inseparable from you,
So may your devotion alone
Be inseparable from me.

10   The path of the senses is threefold,
Marked by pleasure, pain, and delusion.
For the devotee this is the path
That leads to your attainment.

11   The highest state of intellectual knowledge
Has none of the taste of the nectar

* Although the true devotees have overcome the worldly sense of subject-object dualistic perception, they still function as members of ordinary society. Through this perspective, however, the world-as-object becomes Śiva himself; thus the whole world is equated with the body of Śiva.

† Other systems recognize that through deep, fervent meditation a perfect state arises in which the difference between the knower and known dissolves, and the Lord is clearly visible. But for realized devotees he is always clearly visible, even when they are in the normal state of differentiating knower and known, subject and object.

Of your devotion.
To me, O Lord, it is like sour wine.

Those who practice the exalted science   12
Of your devotion
Are the only ones who truly know
The essence of knowledge and ignorance alike.

May this vine of speech,   13
Rising steadily from the root,
Everywhere adorned with blossoms
And sprinkled with the nectar of devotion,
Yield for me fruit abundant with that sentiment.

"One should worship Śiva by becoming Śiva"   14
is the old saying. But the devotees say,
"One should worship Śiva by becoming a devotee."
For they can recognize your essence as nondual,
Even when it is in bodily form.

What for the devoted   15
Does not serve as an instrument
To attain identification with you?
And what, then, for the spiritually inferior,
Does not serve as an obstacle,
Leading to failure in spiritual attainment?

According to *yoga*, you are obtained   16
At particular times and in particular places.
This is deception!
Otherwise, how is it that you appear to devotees,
O Lord, under all conditions?

Pratyāhāra and similar practices   17
Have nothing to do with this unique attainment.
Even in what is merely the yogin's nonmeditative state,
The devotees acquire complete union.*

---

* *Pratyāhāra*, or the withdrawal from objects of the senses, is one of the
requirements of *yoga* for attaining *samādhi*. The devotees, then, enjoy all of the
benefits of *samādhi* without following the established yogic rules of asceticism.

First Song

18   Neither *yoga* nor austerities
Nor ceremonial worship
Is recommended on this path to Śiva.
Here, only devotion is extolled.

19   Within and without, let determinate cognition cease,
Dispelled by the brilliant,
Glowing light of devotion.
Let even the name of anxiety be destroyed
So that I may have direct realization
Of the true nature of all things.

20   With the single word *Śiva*
Ever resting on the tip of the tongue,
The devotees can enjoy
Even the most complete array of savory delights.

21   Who else is to be counted*
By those resting comfortably in the celestial bliss
Of the cool, pure, tranquil, sweet
Sea of the nectar of devotion?

22   Lord! Why should someone like me
Not taste of the *mahauṣadhi*† herb of devotion,
Whose natural extract
Is called liberation?

23   O Lord, the wise pray for those fortunes alone
That nourish the capacity to delight
In the bliss of your devotion.

24   They have experienced inexplicable bliss
In a downpour of devotional nectar.
Even should they fall,
They will not become soiled
With the mire of false attachments
And other such things.

---

* In this state all that exists has merged into one; there is no entity separate from this.

† The *mahauṣadhi* (literally, "very efficacious plant") is an herb valued for its medicinal qualities.

When it ripens, the vine of devotion   25
Inherently bears fruits, called *siddhi*s;
These begin with *aṇimā* and other powers
And culminate in liberation.*

How wonderful it is that the mind, O Lord,   26
In essence the seed of all suffering,
When doused with the nectar of devotion
Bears the magnificent fruit of beatitude.

* The vine, a creeping plant that does not grow straight up but rather winds its way up and down, back and forth, symbolizes devotion; its fruits are the powers that develop inherently as devotion grows. In other verses Utpala warns against undue attachment to these fruits; if one becomes too involved with the lesser powers, which consist of the supernatural manipulation of the natural world (*māyā*, hence "magic"), he becomes caught in the very net (of illusion) that he seeks to control, thereby forfeiting the attainment of the highest power, spiritual liberation.

The Second Song

•

Contemplation of the All-Soul

1   May you be glorified, O Essence of Consciousness,
    Appearing in many forms as Agni,
    The moon, the sun, Brahmā, Viṣṇu,
    The mobile and the immobile.

2   May you be glorified, O Mighty Fire,
    Brilliantly lustrous from smearing the ashes
    That remain of the universe,
    Your sole oblation.

3   May you be glorified, O Mild One,
    Smooth and brimming with the finest nectar,
    O Terrible One who burns away
    The entire universe.

4   May you be glorified, O Mahādeva,
    O Rudra, Śaṅkara, Maheśvara,
    O Śiva, Embodiment of the Mantra.*

5   May you be glorified, O Fire of Śiva,
    O Dreadful One, who,
    Having absorbed the melting fat
    Of the pieces of the three worlds,†
    Remains yet auspicious.

---

* *Embodiment of the Mantra* refers to the universe as a manifestation of the sound
of Śiva (*śivadhvani*).

† Utpala here uses the image of an animal sacrifice.

May the Lord be glorified,   6
The mysterious Śambhu
Whose only definition is that he is
Devoid of all definitions.

Glory to the imperceptible Lord,   7
The antithesis of the Vedas and the Āgamas
And yet the true essence
of the Vedas and the Āgamas.

Glory be to Śambhu,   8
The sole cause of the universe
And its only destroyer,
Who takes worldly form
And who transcends the world.

Glory be to Śambhu,   9
Who is the consummate beginning, middle, and end,
Who takes the form of beginning, middle, and end,
Who is without beginning, middle, or end.

The utterance of your name even once   10
Produces the same effect
As several virtuous deeds.
May you be glorified, O Difficult of Attainment.

Homage to the One who revels always   11
With a band of ghosts
In moving and in nonmoving forms.
May you be glorified, O Skullbearer,
O Essence of Consciousness.

Homage to that wondrous Śambhu,   12
The Deluding One
Who is yet pure and clear;
The Hidden One
Who has yet revealed himself;
The Subtle One
Whose form yet takes the form of the whole universe.

Second Song

13   May you be glorified, O Omnipotent One,
Whose many acts bewilder,
Whose play is to destroy the world
Maintained by Brahmā, Indra, and Viṣṇu.

14   May you be glorified, O Hara,
Fathomless ocean
On whose shores the mere wanderer
Acquires your special powers.*

15   Homage to Śambhu, resplendent lotus
Dwelling unsullied
In the midst of the world's thick mire
Of illusion.†

16   Homage to the Auspicious One,
The Pure, the Protector, the Adorned Soul,
The Beloved, the Highest Truth,
The Best of all things.

17   Homage to Śambhu,
The One who is ever bound
Yet enjoys eternal liberation:
Who is beyond bondage and liberation.

18   In this vast expanse of the three worlds,
Whose whole essence is ludicrous,‡
You are the sole enjoyer of perpetual delight.
May you be glorified, O One without a Second.

19   May you be glorified, O Śarva,
Who are the essence of the "righthanded" path,

---

* The ocean is called *ratnākara*, that is, it produces magical gems that one can acquire only be plunging into its depths. One can obtain the "gems," or powers, of Śiva merely by approaching his "shores"; one need not be immersed in intellectual knowledge nor yogic technique, but must simply approach with a devotional attitude.

† The image of the lotus in mud as representative of the higher or inner self amidst the world of illusion is a well-known image in Indian literature; cf. *Bhagavadgītā* 5.10.

‡ The whole world is ludicrous (*upahāsa*), a joke, the mere play of Śiva. If one identifies with the world, he, too, is ludicrous and without meaning. But if one identifies with Śiva, he obtains the positive aspect of this play, and for him the world becomes a playground of enjoyment.

Who are the essence of the "lefthanded" path,*
Who claim every sect
And no sect at all.

May you be glorified, O Deva,   20
Who can be worshiped in any manner
In any place
In whatever form at all.

May you be glorified, O Granter of Boons,   21
Who are served by those aspiring for liberation,
And whose boundless depths of beauty
Dispel all afflictions.

May you be glorified, O Lord,   22
Who forever fill the three worlds
With infinite beatitude,
Rejoicing in eternal celebration.

Homage to your terrifying sense-goddesses!   23
Whatever they enjoy
Is all in offering to you.

May you be glorified, inaccessible   24
Even to the long-haired sages.
But those endowed with the spirit of devotion
Embrace you without difficulty.

May you be glorified,   25
Vessel of the sweetest nectar,
Treasury of supreme liberation,
Attainable far beyond the farthest limits.

May you be glorified, O Form of the Great *Mantra*,   26
Cool and lucid,
Blessed with exquisite fragrance,
Brimming with the great nectar of immortality.

---

* These names refer to two sects of Tantra commonly known as the *dakṣiṇācāra*
("righthanded path") and *vāmācāra* ("lefthanded path"), referring, by some
interpretations, to the acceptability or dubiousness of their cultic practices.

27   The great cloth
      Representing your absolute oneness
      Is full of the nectar of freedom
      And has not a single spot of color.
      Homage to your teachings, O Lord.*

28   We praise the path of Maheśvara,
      The thunderbolt against all doubts,
      The fire of destruction
      That destroys all misfortune,
      The final dissolution
      Of all things inauspicious.

29   May you be glorified, O Deva!
      Homage! Adoration!
      O Protector of the Whole Universe,
      O Supreme Lord of the Three Worlds,
      For refuge I come to you alone.

---

* The image is of a royal edict or decree (*śāsana*) that is written on a great woven cloth (*mahāpaṭa*). *Śāsana* also denotes a doctrine or teaching; therefore, the doctrine of Śiva is without blemish. In this image the doctrine or edict is full of nectar, yet because its essence is the freedom of Śiva, it is pure and white, without a single spot of color (*citra*) to defile it. *Citra* also denotes a written impression; therefore full understanding of the doctrine comes not through what has been written in speculation but through direct realization.

The Third Song

•

The Gift of Affection

Homage to the miraculous Śambhu, who, 1
Transcending the two forms—the real and the unreal—
Of all that exists,
Constitutes the Third Form.

In this threefold universe of bondage 2
The only ones who are free,
Including the gods and the sages,
Are those who arise from your freedom.

They enjoy perfect happiness 3
Who have the unique elixir
Against the ills of the world:
The remembrance that the entire universe
Is inlaid with your form.

Whose white canopy is the self-illumined moon, 4
Whose fly-whisk is the stream
Of the heavenly Gaṅgā—
He alone is the Supreme Lord.

Bestow on me your glance 5
Which radiates immortal nectar,
Cool and pure
Like a crescent of the moon.

Why, O Lord, do the drops of supreme knowledge 6
That flow from the ocean of your consciousness-bliss

Third Song

Not have the delicious flavor
Of immortal sweetness?

7 Whose heart
Is not immersed in the delight of your nectar,
O Lord,
Has no heart at all.
O Mighty One! He should be despised!

8 Whose heart
Is united with you, O Lord,
Alone is worthy of Śambhu's powers.

9 Meditation on you
Washes away both delights and sorrows
As a river stream
Washes away high lands and low lands alike.*

10 For those who feel no separation from you
And for whom you are dearer than their own souls—
What cannot be said
Of the abundance of their happiness!

11 I roar! Oh, and I dance!
My heart's desires are fulfilled
Now that you, Lord,
Infinitely splendid,
Have come to me.

12 In that state, O Lord,
Where nothing else is to be known or done,
Neither *yoga*
Nor intellectual understanding
Is to be sought after,
For the only thing that remains and flourishes
Is absolute consciousness.†

* Ultimately delights and sorrows amount to the same thing: they are attachments and thus are obstacles to be removed by meditation on Śiva.

† Absolute consciousness (*viśva-eka-pūrṇā*) is the state representing the final oblation of all feelings of separation and multiplicity; on a cosmic level, it is synonymous with world dissolution.

Whose voice ever rings 13
With the eternal sound *Śiva*
Escapes spontaneously
The cruel grip of undefeatable, endless sorrows.

The "first person" 14
Is distinguished from the "second person"
And from the "third person" as well.
You alone are the Great Person,
The refuge of all persons.*

O Lord of the Universe! 15
How lucky are your devotees,
Worthy of being adored by you.
For them, this turbulent ocean of the world
Is like a great pleasure-lake
For their amusement.

Those who delight in you 16
Long for nothing but to identify
With you completely.
How could worldly desires ever be requested!
For the devotees feel ashamed
Even in expressing the prayer:
"May you be revealed to me."

"Higher than Me there is nothing, 17
Yet even then I practice *japa*.
This shows that *japa* is but
Concentration on absolute oneness."
Thus you instruct your devotees
As well as the whole world
Through your *akṣamālā.*†
In essence this is what constitutes *japa*.

---

* Utpala is punning on the grammatical terms of *first, second,* and *third person,* and on the cosmic *Person*; both are expressed by the word *puruṣa*.

† The *akṣamālā* is the string of prayer beads used in *japa* meditation, or repetition of the *mantra*. Here, the unity of Śiva and the devotees is portrayed by the fact that although Śiva is to be worshiped, he is also a worshiper. Cf. 4.25.

Third Song

18   The unreal is indeed different from the real,
And the real is indeed different from that, O Lord!
You are neither real nor unreal,
But the nature of real and unreal both.

19   Though you shine even more brilliantly
Than the rays of a thousand suns
And though you pervade all the worlds,
Still you are not visible.

20   In this unconscious world
You are the form of consciousness.
Among the knowable, you are the knower;
Among the finite, you are the infinite:
You are the highest of all.

21   "No more of these lamentations!"
I cry out loudly before the Lord,
For in spite of knowing all this
I am confused
And I stray from the right path.

The Fourth Song

•

Potent Nectar

You are to be praised, O my mind,   1
For even though you waver,
You worship the protector even of the protectors,
The *guru* of the three worlds,
The beloved of Ambikā.

Although I have gradually traversed   2
The steps of the various gods,
Having as support the feet of Śiva,
What a wonder it is that not even now
Do I part with this lowliest of states!

Show me the inner path!   3
Make disappear completely
The ways of the entire world
So that in an instant, O Lord,*
I may become your servant forever.

O Śiva! Śiva! Śambhu! Śaṅkara!   4
O you who are kind to those seeking refuge,
Have mercy!
For blessings are not at all far away
From the memory of the pair of your lotus feet.

Lord! Reclining on the cushion of your lotus feet,   5
Those who create the world as they like

---

* *In an instant* refers to the practice of *śaktipāta*, whereby the *guru* transmits the power of awakening instantaneously.

Fourth Song

Laugh at Viriñci, who is subordinate
And who is completely smeared
With the soil of his own authority.*

6 Nothing can shine that is separate
From the light of your form, O Lord.
Therefore, though disguised by nature,
You remain accessible.

7 Some people's perceptions become dulled
Because of duality.
But others taste immediately
The brilliant, unbroken body
That is free of duality.

8 O Lord, if that light of yours
Which is smeared with nectar
And which shines to me
Like infrequent flashes of lightning
Could be made more constant,
Then from that time my worship of you
Would also become constant
And nothing else would be required.

9 Just as here it is certain through great insight
That you are everything,
That there is nothing else
Either existent or nonexistent,
So, then, be abundantly evident to me!

10 By your own will, O Lord,
Have I set out on your path.
Why, then, do I behave like ordinary people
Instead of one worthy of you?

11 The sweetest emotion
Blossoms in the hearts of the *cātaka* birds

---

* Even Viriñci (Brahmā), the creator of the world, is dependent upon Śiva. In contrast, the devotees are free to "create" their own worlds, because they have submitted themselves to Śiva instead of seeking independent "authority."

Who long enjoy that blissful experience
When they hear the rumblings of clouds.*

Just through your grace   12
Has this enjoyment increased.
So even when the devotees
Are in a state of separation
Just the mention of you gives rise
To the remembrance of that joy of union.

He who utters the name of Śiva   13,14†
Hundreds and hundreds of times
Grows great through the showering
Of the sweet, sublime nectar.
The marvelous power of this word
Enters even into the hearts of fools.

And that word, which flows like honey
From a nectar-crescent of the moon,
And causes the highest nectar to flow—
That is the sound of Śiva.
Blessed are they who have this sound
Ever on their lips.

This terrible world is about to be ended.‡   15
The deep stain of my mind has melted away.
Still the gates of your city
Are bolted shut
And do not unlatch even slightly.

---

* The *cātaka* is a mythical bird whose sole nourishment is said to be obtained from rain drops. In this image, even the first far-off rumblings of clouds are enough to cause great, lasting joy to the birds, for they are assured of the rain to come. Similarly does the devotee experience bliss just by hearing about Śiva, knowing that absolute joy is to follow.

† Most manuscripts place these two verses together with one long commentary following both. Cf. 10.5,6 and 10.18,19.

‡ This refers to the universal process in which Śiva reabsorbs the whole world into himself. On the microcosmic level, it is the absorption of the individual consciousness into the consciousness of Śiva. This state is not attained without overcoming a stage of tremendous psychic and psychological barriers; the difficult stage of those obstacles, known as *śūnyabhūmi*, is reflected by the exasperated devotee in this verse.

Fourth Song

16   Ardently I desire to behold
Your ever-blossoming lotus face.
O Lord, may you appear to me,
Howsoever faintly,
Face to face.

17   There is no other happiness here in this world
Than to be free of the thought
That I am different from you.
What other happiness is there?
How is it, then, that still this devotee of yours
Treads the wrong path?

18   If I do not continuously sip, with affection,
The wine of the nectar of harmony with you,
Then for a moment I will not be a fitting
Receptacle for your realization.

19   In truth, this person doesn't see
Even the slightest image of your form,
His mind sullied
By the sense of duality.
Even though you are omniscient
And show kindness to your followers
Why do you not hear this cry of mine?

20   Do you remember, O Lord,
That I ever sought after worldly pleasures
Or ever beseeched you for any of them?
Always greatly desired is the nectar
That comes from beholding your form.
That, oh grant me!

21   No sooner had I set foot
On the path of Śiva
Than, through your will,
Hundreds of auspicious things arose for me.
What else could I possibly ask of you, O Lord?

Where the sun, the moon, and all other stars   22
Set at the same time,
There rises the radiant Night of Śiva,
Spreading a splendor of its own.

O Lord of the Gods!   23
Without the taste of nectar from touching your feet,
Even gaining sovereignty in the three worlds
Holds for me no savor at all.

Alas, O Lord, this knot of the soul   24
Prevents your realization.
But fashioned and concealed by you,
That knot is strong indeed—
So strong that, disregarding you,
It slackens not a bit.

O Lord of the Gods!   25
You are an object of incessant worship
By the great ones,
But are yourself a worshiper.
Here in this world
You are an object of vision
From both within and without,
But are yourself a seer.

The Fifth Song

•

The Command of Powers

1   Carry me into your abode, O Lord—
     I, who, through the touch of the *guru**
     Have become attached
     To the pleasure of the touch
     Of your lotus feet.

2   The hair on my head glistens
     With color from the dust of your lotus feet;
     When shall I begin to dance
     The dance of ever-impetuous delight?

3   O Lord! You are my only Lord!
     I perpetually beseech
     That I would sooner be made a mute
     And dwell within you
     Than become wise in any other way.

4   "O Lord! Ocean of Nectar!
     O Gleaming Three-eyed One!
     O Sweet One even of the Monstrous Eyes!"
     Let me cry and dance
     Exclaiming all this with joy.

5   With my eyes closed
     At the touch of your lotus feet,

---

*   Kṣemarāja glosses the term *galepādikayā* as *haṭhaśaktipātakramaḥ*, that is, an advanced stage brought about initially by the touch of the *guru* transmitting the power of Śiva to the devotee, thereby awakening his spiritual awareness.

May I rejoice,
Reeling with drunkenness
From the wine of your devotion.

May I dwell somewhere in a glen   6
Of the mountain of your consciousness
Where lies the uninterrupted state
Of your sublime bliss.

May I live in that sanctuary, O Lord,   7
Where, taking many forms,
You reside with Devī
From the palace up to the city gates.

O Lord, may the rays   8
Of your brilliance beam steadily
Until the lotus of my heart opens
To worship you.

Grant, O Lord,   9
That I fall at your feet always
And find such delight there
That even my mind becomes intoxicated
And dissolves in bliss.

Whether through immense joy or through anguish,   10
Whether from on a wall or in an earthen jug,
Whether from external objects or from within,
Reveal yourself to me, O Lord!

So cool is the nectar   11
From the touch of your lotus feet!
May that always stream through me,
Within and without.

Plunging into the ambrosia-lake   12
Of touching your feet
Is ever for me a pleasure
Beyond all pleasures.

Fifth Song

13   Accept false enjoyment and the other limitations
That I offer unto you, O Lord.
Having transformed them into immortal nectar,
Enjoy them together with the devotees.

14   Contented with your meal
Of the entire world,
Be comfortably seated;
Then bestow on us, your devotees,
Your blessings and your blissful glance.

15   With my eyes closed,
Relishing the wonder of inner devotion,
May I worship even the blades of grass thus:
"Homage to Śiva, my own consciousness!"

16   Having seen the world as consisting of your nature
And having realized the pleasure
Of your nondual form,
Still may I never part
With the enjoyment of the spirit of devotion.

17   O Lord, since you and you alone
Have no wish that is unfulfilled,
Then the fulfillment of your nonduality
Is more than sufficient.

18   May I attain that state
Where one laughs, one dances,
One does away with passion and hatred
And other such things,
And where one drinks
Of the sweet nectar of devotion.

19   May the extraordinary fragrance
Of the blossom of your remembrance
Become fixed in my heart
Until the stench of foul impressions fades away.

20   O Lord, enlighten my heart!
Help me to discriminate between

50

The base delight in false enjoyments
And the superior delight in your lotus feet.

Although I roam about in the states of *yoga*   21
And am not caught up in worldly affairs,
I would rather that my heart tremble,
Intoxicated with the wine of your remembrance.

In speech, in thought,   22
In the perceptions of the mind,
And in the gestures of the body,
May the sentiment of devotion be my companion
At all times, in all places.

Śiva! Śiva! Śiva!   23
Thus is performed the worship
Of constantly repeating your name.
O Lord, may I continue to taste the sweetest nectar,
Which is never repetitious.

May I live, worshiping you   24
In the world made of
Pulsating, endless, consciousness,
Along the path where
All unconsciousness has been dispelled,
In the city made of
Your unfathomable, extraordinary consciousness.

"Nothing at all is of use   25
For becoming firmly established, shining manifest,
Eternally in one's own form."
May this thought take deep root in me,
Purified by the dust of your lotus feet.

When I touch the soles of your feet,   26
It sometimes flashes in my mind
That this whole world
Has merged into a lake of nectar.
Lord! Grant this to me always!

The Sixth Song

•

Tremblings along the Journey

1   Separated from you
Even for an instant, O Lord,
I suffer deeply.
May you always be the subject of my sight.

2   Even if I am separated
From the world of *saṃsāra*
May I not be separated from you,
My beloved.

3   Wherever I go with body, speech, and mind,
Everything that there is, is you alone.
May this highest truth indeed
Become perfectly realized within me.

4   O Lord! Offering you prayers,
May my speech become just as you are:
Beyond all distinctions
And filled with the highest bliss.

5   From the experience of union with you
Let me wander about
Free of every need and desire
Filled with absolute joy
Seeing all of creation as you alone.

6   O Lord, may I perceive the whole world
As filled with you
So much so that I, too,

Be completely satisfied:
Then, no longer will you be bothered
With my entreaties.

Just as cloud droplets are absorbed in the sky,   7
So are the various constituents of the universe
Absorbed in you;
May they always shine visibly for me
As I proceed through the stages
Of spiritual growth.

From the center of the world   8
Let there be visible to me
Your magnificent jewel
That dispells the depths of darkness
With its radiant luster.

On what site do you not dwell?   9
What exists that does not exist in your body?
I am wearied!
Therefore let me reach you everywhere,
Without difficulty.

O Lord, may I realize at will   10
The bliss of embracing your form.
Having attained that,
What have I not accomplished!

Be visible, O Lord!   11
We do not trouble you with other requests.
Anguished, we chase after you.

The Seventh Song

•

Victory over Separation

1   Having found harmony in your sea of bliss
May my heart be rid of this sorry state
Of disharmony
Once and for all.

2   May the axe of faith
In the oneness of your form
Fall on the firm root*
Of false attachments, hatred,
And the other bonds that become manifest as
"This is mine, this is not mine."

3   O Lord, may the chain of the stigmas
Of contradictions perish.
May absolute freedom flash forth in my heart.
May the image made of consciousness
Be flooded with the nectar of bliss.

4   I toss within the egg
Of the world infested with false attachments.
Like a mother, may the devotional sentiment
Nourish me with the sweet essence of bliss
So that I may develop into a bird
With mighty wings.

---

* Here is another image of a plant: not the creeper of devotion, but the hardy weed of false worldly attachments; if allowed to continue its unruly growth, it will wrap around and ensnare the individual soul.

Acquiring the skill to taste the sweet nectar 5
Derived from worshiping your feet,
May these longings of my mind
For the poison of sense objects
Be destroyed in their entirety.

Having been touched 6
By the sunbeams of your devotion,
Let this heart-crystal of mine
Shoot forth the blazing sparks of the passions,
Eradicating them completely.

Forever may I sing my praises 7
Loudly to you,
Located in that place where Hari,
Haryaśva, and Viriñca are waiting outside.*

With the restless joy 8
Born of the rapture of devotion
May I perceive, entirely through the senses,
The whole world in the form of Śiva
And every action to consist of worship.

May my mind be wedded to devotion, 9
And through that union
May children be born
In the form of *aṇimā* and the other powers.
May they mature
So as to strengthen my feeling that
"All these are mine."†

---

* Hari, Haryaśva, and Viriñca are other names for Viṣṇu, Indra, and Brahmā, monumental Vedic gods whose supremacy is challenged by Utpaladeva. The image suggests that the heart of Śiva is a royal chamber where only the devotees can gain access, by merit of their sincerity, not supremacy.

† When the mind (*buddhi*) accepts and "unites" with devotion, *aṇimā* and the other powers of Śiva are produced.

The Eighth Song

•

Unearthly Strength

1   When will that small amount of grace
Abiding with the Lord
And that small amount of devotion
That has come to me
Unite to become like that unique form—
The blissful body of Śiva?

2   Here in this world
May there arise in me continually
The blissful experience of the highest fulfillment
That comes from your supremacy.
May *jñāna, yoga,* and powers such as *aṇimā*
Remain afar.

3   Let me, like other people,
Yearn deeply for the objects of the world,
But allow me to view them as your form,
O Lord, without contradiction.*

4   In the different stages
Of the growth of the body,
In the modifications of the mind,
In the many situations
On the path of life,
Reveal to me your own blissful form.

---

* In the state of *īśvarapratyabhijñā* one can experience fully the pleasures of the world as well as the pleasures of uniting with Śiva, without feeling a contradiction between "worldly" and "other-worldly."

Let the sense faculties, full of delight,   5
Be attached to their respective objects.
But may there not be, even for an instant,
Any loss of the joy
Of your nonduality.

As I become absorbed within you,   6
Experiencing your form—so light,
Mild, clear, and cool—
May I transcend that behavior of ordinary life
Dependent upon material objects.

May my body blossom into your true nature,   7
The worlds become my limbs.
May all this dualistic feeling
Be forgotten forever,
Even after crossing into the realm of memory.

From the vision of your face   8
May there arise for me
A flood of the highest nectar
So that the terrible cavern
Obscuring my realization of your form
Be filled in completely.

Whenever I am sprinkled with even a few drops   9
Of the nectar of your touch
I become indifferent to
All the pleasures of the world.
Why must I be deprived of both types of pleasures?*

O Unborn One!   10
May I, the royal swan perpetually gliding
Across the lake of your lotus feet,
Reach the top, middle, and indeed the root
Of the lotus stalk of devotion.

---

* At this point the devotee has discerned that mundane endeavors alone are not
sufficient, and he becomes less and less content with a solely worldly basis in life. But
with only intermittent experience of joyful spiritual union, he is left unable to derive
complete satisfaction from either path.

Eighth Song

11   May there exist, O Lord,
All the objects of my thought and my sight.
But may each of them blossom
As the bliss of vision, reflection,
And illumination.

12   O Mightiest Lord!
Even when there is a deluge of those miseries
May I not only be free from fear,
But may I also enjoy the blissful, supreme
Exultation at the touch of your body.

13   While woven into your being
This entire universe
Is also projected outward.
I have come to understand this
Through strong determination;
May I realize it also
Through sensual experience.

The Ninth Song

•

The Triumph of Freedom

When shall my heart, anxiously longing   1
For a new experience of tender devotion,
Abandon all else
And come to touch you?

Of you alone enamored,   2
Having as my only treasure
The worship of your feet,
When shall I make you visible, O Lord,
Before these very eyes?

When shall my mind   3
Indifferent to all else through love's intensity
Tear open the great door latch
With a loud bang
And finally arrive in your presence, O Lord?

Through the power of your devotion, O Lord,   4
When shall I overcome all of the gods
Who reside in my heart,
The core of consciousness?

When shall I enjoy the bounteous celebration   5
Of the rapture of devotion,
Where the elements of the objective world
Become filled with the bliss of consciousness?

When shall that moment come, O Lord,   6
When all of a sudden I recognize you,

Ninth Song

The Fearless, Exalted, Whole, Without Cause,
The One, indeed, to have veiled himself—
And in so doing make you ashamed?

7 When, O Lord, shall I become
Such a cherished devotee of yours
That you never consider it appropriate
To run away from me?

8 Viewing all creatures as immersed in your worship—
When shall I retain this vision,
And be flooded with its sweet, delightful nectar?

9 When shall my yearning for devotion—
The highest state of knowledge and
The highest stage of *yoga*—
Become fulfilled, O Lord?

10 When shall I become helplessly enraptured
And reveal to everyone my joy,
Having suddenly obtained and firmly clasped
The treasure of your most precious feet?

11 When, O Lord, shall I possess
Your pure, far-reaching radiance
So that never may I become sullied
By the shadow of *māyā*?

12 Having assimilated into myself this orb of the world,
And free of all desires,
When, O Lord, shall I become prominent
In the community of your devotees?

13 Of the pride in the world,
You are the one cause.
Bursting with the spirit of your devotion,
When shall I attain the Great Pride?

14 Replete with all objects, embraced by Śrī,*

* Śrī is one of the names of the goddess of wealth, here, according to Kṣemarāja,
representative of the wealth of devotion.

When shall I comfortably take my rest
At the pair of your soothing lotus feet?

When shall I, flushed with the wine of devotion,   15
Reach the limits of joy in your worship,
Attaining the highest fulfillment, O Lord?

When shall I have the bliss of your touch   16
So that I stammer and lose my voice,
Choking on streams of blissful tears,
With peals of laughter abloom on my face?

When, O Lord, shall I shake off   17
This habit of acting like brutish people*
So that I enjoy an attitude
Befitting your devotees?

Having attained *aṇimā* and the other powers   18
And having overcome all fears of distress,
When shall I lose myself in the pastime
Of drinking that magical, life-giving draft?

When, O Lord, shall my voice   19
Produce such a lament
That your image flashes suddenly before my eyes?

With my heart set on   20
Tightly embracing your lotus feet,
When shall I behold you without any effort
In the form of being and nonbeing both?

---

* *Paśujana* ("brutish, beastly people") carries the implication of the state of the
bonded soul, called *paśu*. As lord of all people, of all beasts (especially wild ones), and
indeed of all bonded souls, Śiva bears the epithet *Paśupati*.

The Tenth Song

•

Breaking the Continuity

1 Surely you, the sole presiding deity of the universe,
Should not tolerate the followers of Maheśvara
Behaving like the ordinary people of the world.

2 Those who, through never-ending affection
Have become the followers of your feet,
Derive the deepest pleasures
From anything that they do.

3 Where you, the Great Destroyer, are protector,
How can there be any disease?
Wherever your Lakṣmī* resides,
What other desire for enjoyment can there be?

4 Whoever should obtain the all-pervading Lord
For just a moment's happiness
Becomes filled with your bliss for all time,
Even from that very instant.

5,6 The moon is a drop of the nectar of your bliss
That has trickled down to earth,
Just as the sun is a mere particle
Of your brilliant light, O Lord.

We dedicate ourselves to this,
Your third eye,
The one symbol of your transcendental mystery.

* Kṣemarāja comments that the goddess of wealth here represents "the accomplishment of the splendor of nonduality."

Who is much exalted, beholding you   7
Has truly your realization.
Who is struck suddenly with ineffable joy—
He too has your realization.

Having gotten into your heart, O Lord,   8
Those granted with your grace
Have withdrawn the exterior world from you
And merged it within the interior.

Everything else except you, O Lord,   9
Has two eyes—that is, even—eyes.
But you, the only Lord of the world,
Are of the uneven eyes.*

Without you, your opponents†   10
Would not be able to speak ill of you.
Even their disparaging remarks
Would not exist but through your majesty.

If, O Lord, there be in my heart   11
A place for you that is free
Of inner and outer obstacles—
What else then would be needed?

Some wander about from birth to birth,   12
Utterly restless souls.
Others, Lord, move throughout the world,
Joyously equipoised.

Without having drunk of the nectar of your devotion   13
And without having beheld your essence,
Even then do people become perfected
By merely hearing about you, O Lord.

We are your servants, O Lord!   14
Therefore we should receive the same care from you
As you foster on the soul of the three worlds.

* *Uneven* refers to the three eyes of Śiva; it also connotes "odd, terrible, monstrous,"
thus the fearsome aspect of Śiva.

† Kṣemarāja glosses these as Buddhists, Sāṃkhyas, Mīmāṃsakas, and so forth.

Tenth Song

15   Having seen you, the soul of the world,
      Made of the nectar of the highest bliss,
      Even now do I yet more intensely
      Long for the ecstacy of your touch.

16   All misfortunes suffered by those of the world
      Become tolerable
      When joined with that form of yours
      Known as constancy.

17   With you existing as the essence of consciousness,
      Omniscient and omnipotent,
      The manifestation of this world—
      Appearing as false in every respect—
      Is understood as your true form.

18,19 Enlivened by you, these senses quiver
      Though they be like lumps of clay.
      They dance, like feathery fluffs of cotton
      Raised up by the breeze.

      If, O Lord, the senses were not
      Endowed with self-consciousness,
      Then who would forsake the realization
      That the world is one with you?

20   They are to be praised, O Supreme Lord,
      Who, while yet in the state of dissolution
      Have been purified
      By the touch of the fire of your wrath.*

21   Though you stand completely manifest
      With a body of splendrous light,
      Why do I wander about, O Lord,
      In darkness?

22   You, the indivisible Lord, are my immortal form.
      Yet still, I am only an abode
      Of mortal characteristics.

* This refers to the demons who were killed by Śiva; the touch of Śiva's fire, though wrathful, brings more merit than not being touched at all.

Whose speech is adorned   23
With the name *Maheśvara*
And whose forehead bears the mark
Of salutation,
Is indeed alone the exalted one.

Since you indeed are real and unreal   24
Why then do I not realize you
Without any effort,
Spontaneously?

For a servant of Śiva   25
Who has identified himself with Śiva,
What happiness is there that cannot be attained?
Therefore even the heads of the gods
Serve me the wine of immortality.

Between the heart and the navel of living beings,   26
In the form of the great digestive fire*
You devour all
That moves and moves not.

---

* Here, through his power of *mahimā*, Śiva has expanded his body so as to consume easily everything in the world; the digestive fire of individual living beings is the same conflagration that annihilates the universe.

The Eleventh Song

•

Bound to the World by Desire

1 Neither this world
Nor a friend
Nor a relative
Belongs to me at all.
When you are all this
Who else then could be mine?

2 You, O Master, are the Great Lord.
You are in truth the entire world.
Thus, asking for any one specific thing
Is just the asking
And nothing more.

3 Supremacy over the three worlds appears
As trifling as a piece of straw
To those who are devoted to you.
What other fruit than your remembrance
Need their good deeds bear?

4 When nothing at all is different from you
And even the creator of the worlds
Is your creation,
There is no need, then, to sing the praises
Of your miraculous deeds.

5 I am one with you,
Constantly immersed in worshiping you.
Since I am like this all the time,

Why can I not realize it naturally
Even when I am dreaming?

Those who have gotten just a whiff   6
Of the fragrance, however slight,
Of your lotus feet—
To them all things of enjoyment,
Even those much desired by the gods,
Appear putrid.

It isn't the case   7
That there is one thing in your heart,
Another in your speech,
And yet another in your actions.
Be clear, O Śambhu!
Bestow either grace or punishment.

I am confused, overcome with sorrow.   8
Old age and infirmities terrify me.
My strength gone, I come to you for shelter.
Therefore, grant, O Śambhu, that before long
The highest of all states be reached by me,
Far beyond the path of pain.

When they reach your ears   9
My laments, however meager,
Become precious
Like the drops of rain
That one by one,
Falling in the core of the bamboo shoot,
Become pearls.*

What, O Lord, is not attained   10
By those people who even for a moment pretend
To be devoted to your name?
O bearer of the crescent moon on your head,
Allow that, vanquishing death,
I may attain *aṇimā* and the other powers.

---

* This refers to a phenomenon said to occur on the day of Divālī, when the sun and
moon both are in the Svāti Nakṣatra (constellation of the star Arcturus).

Eleventh Song

11   O Śambhu, O Śarva,
    Bearer of the crescent moon on your head,
    O Śiva, O Three-eyed One,
    Bearer of the Prayer Beads, O Venerable One,
    Having Horrifying Skulls as your Symbol,
    O Brilliant One,
    Having Fearsome Trident as your Weapon,
    O Ocean of Compassion, O Ferocious Power,
    Creator of the Three Worlds, O Śrīkaṇṭha!
    Quickly annihilate all of this inauspiciousness
    And bestow on me the highest perfection.

12   What, O Master, could exist,
    Whose creator is not the Lord?
    What does a sentient being experience
    That is not due to the great, immutable
    Powers of Śaṅkara?
    I ever abide in you,
    But even so I am constantly depressed,
    Struggling with mental agonies.

13   O Granter of Boons, here in this world
    Inevitable are pain, old age, and death.
    But leave these aside for a moment:
    Even the highly esteemed Sound itself
    And other such things are ephemeral.
    Even so, I long for everlasting happiness,
    For the enduring, eternal elixir of life—
    The sweet meditation on your lotus feet.

14   O Master, expert at vanquishing
    The miseries of devotees,
    Treasure of auspiciousness,
    Having matted locks—
    Now, when I am an abode only of pain,
    Grant me the highest perfection of your worship
    While I am still living
    And fit for the sweetest of pleasures.

15   May he be glorified
    Whose eternal activity

Is the destruction of the great veil of illusion,
Whose symbol is the moon,
Whose light outshines all other lights.

The Twelfth Song

•

Particulars of the Arcane Lore

1   Everything is saturated with you alone.
Why, when this is the case, O Lord,
Do you not reveal yourself,
Even now?

2   You are dominant
In worldly objects,
In the various sense organs,
And when I am enlightened with knowledge.
Even while you permeate all of these things
You are beyond them.
May I have that revelation at all times.

3   Those who proceed on the path of beholding you
Are fortunate to have your blessings.
How can they be reborn
And how can they be known by anyone?
They are decorated
With the naturally glorious symbol.
You lift them up again and again
From ordinary things in their worldly life—
From water, from grass, and from other things—
And you fill them with waves of nectar.

4   Satiated with the nectar
Flowing from the direct realization of your form,
Having eradicated desire,
Intoxicated,
They wander about at their will.

Neither "then" nor "always"   5
Nor even "once."
Where no perception of time exists,
That very thing is your realization.
And it can neither be called eternal nor anything else.

With my heart pining for your vision   6
May I only attain this much power through *yoga*:
That by merely wishing it
I may gain entrance to the innermost sanctuary
To perform your worship.

With minds blossomed   7
From attaining an unwavering vision of you,
The actions and words of devotees
Are flawless—naturally.*

O Lord, may my permanent abode   8
Be at your feet
And may I be fearless.
Whatever my station in the world
May I worship you
With actions unrestricted.

Having completely entered   9
Your lotus feet,
Having lost all desires,
Let me consume the most bounteous honey
And wander about at will,
Completely satisfied.†

Even for him whose thought of worshiping you   10
Arises only hypocritically,
Inevitably he acquires an appropriate
Closeness to you.

---

* Kṣemarāja adds that the true devotees have the natural ability to raise the spiritual standards of those around them.

† The image here is the typically Indian one of a bee entering a flower; entering the lotus that represents the body of Śiva, the wanderer finds nothing but endless honey.

Twelfth Song

11   O Lord, indifferent to everything else,
With only one delight in my heart,
Shall I ever drink enough of the Lord,
Who is easily accessible,
Who is all-calming?

12   Separated from you,
All this, whatever it may be,
Should be rejected.
And everything consisting of you
Should be accepted.
This, in short, is the essence
(Of all spiritual wisdom).

13   The objective world,
Moving about within you,
Is to be adored.
So then, outside of you, Lord,
How can nonexistence be conceived of,
Much less adored?

14   O Three-eyed One!
Transcending speech and empirical knowledge,
Let me, without obstacles,
Behold only you, Lord,
Everywhere, all the time,
Even when emotionally agitated.*

15   Reveal, O Deva, your abode
Where you ever reside with Parameśvarī.
Those who abide
In the midst of the dust of the Master's feet—
Are such servants unreliable?

16   Even having come along
On the path of seeing you,
Why, my Lord, do you elude your servant?

---

* In other spiritual paths this realization is said to occur only during a state of equipoise.

For what creature here on earth
Do you not present yourself for a moment?*

Inundated with the pure,   17
Endlessly flowing stream of nectar
Of the supreme knowledge
That all is one,
When, O Lord, shall I realize absolute identification
Between you and my physical form,
And obtain neverending bliss?

So that I may become your worshiper,   18
Let me attain just the smallest share
Of the essence of that insight
Into how the world becomes bound up in misery.

Every moment, while beholding different objects,   19
Let me clearly see you and you alone, O Lord,
As assuming the form of the whole universe.

Why does my mind not view   20
The various objects of my desire
As not different from the limbs of your body?
In so doing, it would not lose its nature
And my highest desire would also be realized.

Hundreds indeed are those, O Lord,   21
Who through your inspiration
While living the lives of average people
Perceive just through these very eyes
Your form ever before them.

Not a thought arises   22
That does not constitute your will.
All acts, favorable or otherwise,
Are always performed by the Lord himself.
Thus abiding in you, I wander through the world

---

* Kṣemarāja points out that in some form or another, Śiva presents himself before
every living thing. The servant, however, expects special consideration because of his
closeness to the Master.

Twelfth Song

With nothing to frustrate the festival
Of the worship of your spotless feet.

23   May insight into your mysterious language
Dawn on me completely.
May I develop such power
That worshiping you incessantly
Becomes a habit.

24   Let even my various worldly concerns
Always appear to me thus:
As part of you, and therefore not worthy
In and of themselves.

25   While my mind wanders of its own inclinations
Here and there in the range of the senses,
Let me become in your worship, O Lord,
An adept unwavering.

26   Through your will alone was I born your servant—
Through no other force.
Even then, why am I never blessed
With the vision of your countenance?
How strange!

27   Those who long for you intensely
Discover you in every object.
Oh, what spiritual path do they follow
That has yielded them this fruit?

28   May all objects, Your Majesty,
Appear to me as truly embodying your being.
Let nothing else
Mean a thing to me.

29   Whatever is not,
Let that be nothing to me.
Whatever is,
Let that be something to me.
In this way may it be

That you be found and worshiped by me
In all states.

The Thirteenth Song

•

In Summary . . .

1   Hear in summary, O Lord,
What defines my joy and my sorrow:
Union with you is joyousness;
Separation, deep agony.

2   There is, within me,
The tiniest dark spot
That keeps you hidden.
Completely wiping away even that,
Reveal, O Lord, your spotless form.

3   In whatever state of being—
Life, death, or anything else—
May I worship you constantly
In your imperishable body
That embraces the whole world
And consists of the bliss of eternal consciousness.

4   I am the Lord.
I, indeed, am the Handsome One,
The Learned One, the Fortunate.
Who else is there in the world
Like me?
Such a splendid feeling
Befits only your devotees.

5   Therefore with the consciousness
Of the true essence of things
That emanates from the removal of

The obstacles to the nectar of your nonduality,
Make me worthy, O Lord of the Gods,
Of the worship of your feet.

Let there be that great festival of worship   6
Where the Supreme Lord himself
Is meditated upon, seen, and touched.
Be always mine through your grace.

The realization of things as they really are   7
And the supreme festival of your worship—
One is intertwined with the other,
And they always blossom
In those who are filled with devotion.

While incessantly drinking in through the senses   8
The heady wine of your worship
From the overflowing goblets of all objects,
Let madness overtake me.

Where not even a trace   9
Of otherness exists,
Where self-luminosity is everywhere manifest,
There, in your city,
Let me reside
Forever as your worshiper.

It is by your own will, O Supreme Lord,   10
That I hold a position as your servant.
Why, then, am I not deserving to behold you
Or even of the task of pressing your feet?*

Lord, although it is fitting,   11
You never discriminate
When bestowing grace.
What has befallen me now that you delay
In revealing a glimpse of yourself?

* In India pressing the feet is a type of massage typically reserved for a low member
of the household hierarchy to perform on a high-ranking member (as a young child on
a grandparent, or the youngest daughter-in-law on the family matriarch); it indicates
subservience and respect.

Thirteenth Song

12   Worshiping you with my own hands,*
Let me behold you, together with Parameśvarī,
Shining in all things exterior and interior,
Ever filling the three worlds.

13   Having ascended to the Master's palace
By sheer intent,
Without obstruction,
Let me always enjoy the sweetest bliss
Of drinking the immortal wine of your grace.

14   That which bestows on all objects of beauty
The property of giving wonder at the mere touch—
By that very principle do those endowed with
Unwavering devotion
Worship your form.

15   Being self-luminous
You cause everything to shine;
Delighting in your form
You fill the universe with delight;
Rocking with your own bliss
You make the whole world dance with joy.

16   He who without hesitation
Views all of this tangible world as your form,
Having filled the universe
With the form of his own self,
Is eternally joyful.
Why, then, the fear?

17   Even the deadly poison
That rests in a corner of your throat, O Lord,
Is supreme nectar to me.
Nectar that is separate from your body,
Even if easily accessible,
Doesn't interest me.

---

* Kṣemarāja notes that this implies the dedication of the individual self to the cosmic self; the "hands" refer to *mudrā*s, or hand gestures, one of the "five distinguishing marks" (*pañcalakṣaṇa*) of Tantric worship.

May my countenance be ever flushed with excitement 18
From talking and singing about you.
And may I ever be blessed with the desire
To perform your worship of love.

Oh, the ways of the Supreme Lord 19
Cannot be reckoned!
He has presented me his own being,
Bursting with sweet, immortal nectar,
But yet does not allow me
To drink.

Entering you, my own being, 20
The fathomless, the undifferentiated,
The one without a second,
Devouring all sense of (subject and) object,
O Lord of Umā,
Ever may I worship and sing praises of you.

The Fourteenth Song

•

Song of Glorification

1   In the presence of my Master,
Repository of the most magnificent wealth,
Let me relish the nectar
Of chanting glorifications again and again.

2   May you be glorified, the one Rudra,
The one Śiva, the Great God, The Great Lord,
Beloved of Pārvatī,
Firstborn of All the Gods.

3   May you be glorified, Lord of the Three Worlds,
Bearing on your forehead the unique third eye.
May you be glorified, who bear on your throat
The mark of deadly poison,
Having swallowed the afflictions of the afflicted.

4   May you be glorified, in whose hand glistens
The sharp trident symbolic of the three powers.*
May you be glorified,
Whose most venerable lotus feet
Can fulfill a desire the moment it arises.

5   May you be glorified, whose transcendental form
Radiates manifold splendor.
May you be glorified, whose forehead bears ashes
And in a single tuft of whose hair
Flows the stream of Gaṅgā.

---

* The three powers are *icchā* (will, desire), *jñāna* (knowledge), and *kriyā* (action).

May you be glorified, anointed with moonlight   6
Reflected in the vast ocean of milk.
May you be glorified, O Lord whose ornaments
Are snakes dazzling with jewels
Begotten at your touch.

May you be glorified, O worthy refuge   7
Of the only immortal crescent of the moon.*
May you be glorified, ever consecrated
As the lord of the universe
With the waters of Gaṅgā.

May you be glorified, the mere touch of whose feet   8
Has made sacred the entire bovine family.
May you be glorified, who always appear
At the gatherings of devotees.

May you be glorified, who through your own will   9
Deceive fools by assuming ascetic disguise.
May you be glorified, who enjoy the deserved
Propitious fortune of Gaurī's embrace.

May you be glorified, who delight in offerings   10
Drenched in the sentiment of devotion.
May you be glorified, pleased with the singing
And dancing of devotees drunk on your wine.

May you be glorified, who bring about   11
The birth and death of the powers
Of Brahmā and the other lords of the gods.
May you be glorified, whose orders are carried out
By the ranks of the lords of the universe.

May you be glorified,   12
Who have made manifest your grandeur
By placing your signet
On each and every thing in the world.
May you be glorified, Great Lord,

---

* Kṣemarāja notes that of the sixteen crescents of the moon, Śiva has given refuge
only to that of the new moon, which is called Amā. The new moon is thus, by its
connection with Śiva, considered immortal and is observed by Śaivas as a sacred time.

Lord of the universe into which
You have infused your own soul.

13   May you be glorified, who are without second
When the will arises to create the three worlds.
May you be glorified, whose only assistant is
Devī, treasury of all of your powers.

14   May you be glorified, who permeate
All the three worlds simultaneously.
May you be glorified, whose sound, *Īśvara*,
Is never despised, not even by fools.

15   May you be glorified, whose innate supremacy
Depends neither on compassion nor other virtues.
May you be glorified, whose unique, destructive powers
Destroy even the Great Death.*

16   May you be glorified, unobstructed
In bringing about universal annihilation.
May you be glorified, the chanting of whose name
Is followed by a thousand auspicious qualities.

17   May you be glorified, who without the slightest effort
Gave away this ocean of nectar.†
May you be glorified, a moment of whose wrath
Sets the universe in flames.

18   May you be glorified,
The only lamp for worldly beings
Blinded by the darkness of delusion.
May you be glorified, O Supreme Person,
Ever awake in the midst of a sleeping world.

19   May you be glorified, a partridge warbling
Within the mountain grove of my body.

---

* The Great Death represents time (*kāla*), that is, mortality.

† This refers to the story of Upamanyu, who was a child so poor that he had to drink rice water instead of milk; nonetheless he trusted in Śiva despite all hardships. Pleased with such steadfast devotion, Śiva bestowed on the child the whole cosmic ocean of churning milk.

May you be glorified, most excellent swan
Gliding through the skies
Of the minds of devotees.

May you be glorified, lord of the   20
Mountain of gold and other precious metals.
May you be glorified, an inauspicious moon
That descends like a meteor
Upon those who defy you.*

May you be glorified, difficult of attainment   21
For ascetics and gods pained by harsh austerities.
May you be glorified, easily attainable
By the community of devotees in every state.

May you be glorified, who have   22
Made worthy of a stream of fortunes
Those who seek refuge in you.
May you be glorified, whose only purpose
Is to lovingly care for
Those who have come to you.

May you be glorified, outstanding   23
As the one causative factor in the creation,
Preservation, and destruction of the world.
May you be glorified, O great joy of Utpala,
Whose work is rendered as sheer delight
Through the madness of devotion.

May you be glorified, O Worthy of Devotion!   24
May you be glorified,
Conqueror of birth, old age, and death.
May you be glorified, O World Patriarch!
Glory, glory, glory, glory,
Glory, glory, glory, glory,
Glory, glory, glory, glory,
Glory, O Three-eyed Lord!

---

* That is, for those who are not your devotees, even the moon, which represents
auspiciousness itself, becomes inauspicious; thus it becomes like a meteor, a
destructive, rather than auspicious, celestial entity.

The Fifteenth Song

•

About Devotion

1   There are scriptures that can cleanse a person
Of the three impurities.*
And there are those yogins and pandits
Who have mastered these scriptures.
But the only ones truly equipoised
Are those devoted to you.

2   Well satisfied with the food
Of *kāla, niyati, rāga,* and
The other coverings of *māyā,*†
The devotees wander joyfully, O Lord,
Along the shores of the world.

3   Whether weeping or laughing, they address you
In loud, delirious speech.
Uttering hymns of praise, the devoted
Are truly unique attendants.

4   My wish is to be neither an ascetic
Indifferent to the world
Nor a manipulator of supernatural powers
Nor even a worshiper craving liberation—
But only to become drunk
On the abundant wine of devotion.

---

*   The three "impurities" (*malas*) are *āṇava, māyīya,* and *kārma.*

†   There are five "coverings" (*kañcukas*) of *māyā: kāla* (time), *niyati* (pervasiveness of space), *rāga* (enjoyment), *vidyā* (knowledge), and *kalā* (authorship).

84

I bow to him who,   5
Drawing the outside world into his heart,
Worships you, O Lord,
With streams of the nectar of devotion.

Amidst righteousness and unrighteousness,   6
Amidst works and knowledge,
Amidst prosperity and hardship,
Your devotees, in the face of all this,
Enjoy the bliss of your devotion.

O Master, father of the mobile and immobile,   7
Even the blind and the leprous
Look exceedingly graceful
When adorned with your supreme devotion.

O Lord, those who are filled   8
With the great warmth of devotion,
Although pale in body,
And having husks of grain as a bed
And as clothing the feathers of birds,
Dominate even over the Lord of Wealth.*

As they ascend to you   9
Rolling, immersed in the nectar of your devotion,
A few, O Lord, worship you
With their whole being
Through their hearts.

O Lord, it is worthy of   10
Protection, support, and high esteem—
This great wealth of your devotion,
Which removes the troubles of the world.

Although your community of devotees, Lord,   11
Is passionately attached to you,

---

* The Lord of Wealth is Kubera, himself a great devotee of Śiva.

Fifteenth Song

May Svāminī, leaving envy behind,
Be ever pleased with them.*

12   Once there is devotion to you,
Union with you is certain.
Once a large pitcher of milk has been obtained,
Vain is a concern about yogurt.†

13   Is this not an unparalleled *siddhi*;
Does it not cause supreme bliss to flow?—
This increasing devotion to Śambhu
That becomes everlasting.

14   Alas, submerged in my darkened mind
The exquisite jewel of your devotion
Does not manifest the innate, sublime
Flashes of its own splendor.

15   Devotion to you, Master of the Three Worlds,
Is indeed the supreme *siddhi*.
But without *aṇimā* and the other powers,
Even that, O Lord, is not perfect.
This is my anguish.

16   Emitting the sweet fragrance of *Śiva* flowers,
Which blossom within and without,
The yogins perfume even those of ill habits
Who come into their presence.‡

---

* In a playful mood, Utpala entreats Śiva's wife not to be jealous of the passionate relationship between her husband and his devotees, who are here referred to as a feminine entity, *janatā* ("community").

† That is, all one needs to produce yogurt is enough milk, and similarly, the "recipe" for union with Śiva is an ample supply of devotion. The added implication is of an initial spark, or something obtained in the way of divine grace, necessary to initiate the process, just as yogurt requires an initial starter culture.

‡ The notion that highly attained beings emit a sweet fragrance is well known. *Śiva* flowers (*tryambakastavaka*) are the fragrant blossoms of a plant of the nightshade family known in Sanskrit as *dhattūra* and in Latin as *Datura alba*; with its poisonous and narcotic qualities and white blossoms, the plant is identified with Śiva and is used in his worship. Thus, in this verse the yogins also emit the essence of Śiva himself.

Where not even the notion of light exists,   17
Where the whole world remains asleep,
There, in that state of Śivarātri,*
The devotees, without pause, O Lord,
Honor you in worship.

Let *sattva* shine forth in the worship of Śiva,   18
Lord of the True Qualities.
Let heaps of dust from Lord Śaṅkara's feet
Shine as *rajas* on my head.
Let *tamas* flourish and completely destroy
The impressions of memory and the other attachments.
Thus, Lord, may the three *guṇas* as a unit
Merge together with your being.†

Endless is the cycle of birth and death.   19
These slender limbs are consumed
By diseases harsh and diverse.
I have derived no real enjoyment
From pleasures of the senses.
What happiness encountered was not long lasting.
Thus, my existence has become useless.
Grant me, O Lord,
Those sublime and everlasting treasures
So that I may become your devotee
With my head illumined by touching the feet
Of the One adorned with the moon.

---

* Śivarātri ("Night of Śiva") is a pan-Indian festival celebrated on the thirteenth day of the dark fortnight of the lunar month Phālguna. Here, Utpala transforms the external festival into an internal celebration of transcendental union.

† The three *guṇas* ("qualities") are *sattva* (equanimity, lightness), *rajas* (energy, redness), and *tamas* (slothfulness, darkness). In various combinations they characterize human personality and inclination. The full workings of the *guṇas* together indicate immersion in the world of *saṃsāra*. Other Indian systems advocate withdrawing from the *guṇas*, at least those of *tamas* and *rajas*, but Utpala sees the merit in each of these qualities not only to be incorporated into the spiritual quest, but indeed to strengthen it. This is done by dedicating one's whole, complex personality to Śiva, and asking that he take the *guṇas* into himself for the proper transformation.

The Sixteenth Song

•

Breaking out of the Fetters

1   What indeed is there in the world
    That does not conceal you?
    Yet nothing exists that can conceal
    You from the devotees.

2   Attained by so many disciples
    And with so many attributes
    You appear at all times to the devotees
    In your true form, O Lord.

3   Triumphant, they laugh,
    And vanquished, they laugh even more—
    Those select few who are maddened
    With the immortal wine of your devotion.

4   Let me delight in the sweet, sublime
    Bliss of your devotion,
    Leaving behind not only base powers,
    But liberation itself.

5   In the same way that it arose in me,
    Allow this love of devotion
    Previously unknown to me
    To grow greater still, O Lord.

6   Truly, I have no other entreaty but this:
    Let me for all time, O Lord,
    Be consumed with unending devotion.

Let me be enraged and yet 7
Compassionate toward the world.
And thus in the madness of devotion
May I laugh and weep and chant
Śiva, thunderously.

Under the spell of devotion, O Lord, 8
Let me be inconstant yet at peace,
Mournful yet laughing,
Distracted yet aware.

Whether within or without, 9
Your devotees know you
As the embodiment of consciousness.

Though pretending to listen 10
To the words of blasphemers,
And with needle-like sensations prickling the skin,
Enraptured still are the devotees
With drops of delicious nectar.

However painful a sensation, 11
It is transformed into a means of enjoyment
For devotees whose consciousness
Is suffused with the moonlight nectar.*

Living in whatever state, 12
The devotees enjoy—both within and without—
The sublime bliss
Of the touch of your being.

A chosen few, O Lord, surpass 13
Plaintiveness when worshiping you,
And enjoy your spotless, immortal form.

The knowers of *śāstras* become deluded 14
And thus become estranged:
Indeed, delusion produces estrangement.

---

* The moonlight nectar is the bliss emanating from Parāśakti.

Sixteenth Song

But you appear for devotees
As the one, unrivaled truth.

15   How can he be like other people—
The devotee with mind made pure
By exhausting fame and infamy,
Attachment and aversion?

16   What position do the followers
Of the path of knowledge
Hold over these great souls
Who have vanquished the gloom of attachment and aversion
With the bright light of your devotion?

17   Whose worship consists
Of bathing in and drinking of
The nectar of devotion
Finds rest in the transcendental peace
Of the first, middle, and last stages.

18   You alone are the subject
Of their songs and speculations,
You, the subject of their quests and their worship.
Laudable, then, is the devotee's pilgrimage of life
Lived in harmony with you.

19   What is called liberation
Is simply the ripeness of devotion, O Lord.
Having taken the first steps toward that,
We are even now almost liberated.

20   With my mind spilling over with your devotion,
Let any difficulty come my way.
But should I feel separate from you,
I would not want
Even an endless chain of happiness.

21   You are pleased, O Lord, with devotion.
And devotion arises at your will.
You alone understand
How these are connected.

Having a form or formless,   22
Within or without,
In every way, O Lord,
You are the embodiment of immortality
For those who are drunk with your devotion.

Here in this world   23
Another world exists
That bears as fruit joyousness
For your devotees.

May there be devotion to you   24
As the Secret One, as the Transcendent One,
As Lord of the Universe,
As Śambhu, as Śiva,
As the Celestial One.
Ah, how indeed could I ever express it?

Devotion, devotion, devotion   25
To the Transcendent One.
Ardent devotion!
This is why I cry and clamor!
Let me have ardent devotion for you,
Only you.

You are the fountainhead, O Lord,   26
Of everything beautiful.
All things become precious at your touch,
Whether gem or piece of straw.

Not separating themselves from you   27
When experiencing, through the senses,
The subject and object—
They indeed are your true devotees.

Some, O Lord, embrace you   28
Outside of world society.
Others forego all the rules,
And through the warmth of devotion
Embrace you in the midst of the world.

Sixteenth Song

29   I honor Śiva, who
During the festival of the world's dissolution
Is passionately and intensely held by Śivā,*
Through whom the whole universe is enjoyed
By means of drinking, eating, and embellishments.

30   O Lord of the Universe,
Glorious is your sovereignty!
Similarly glorious is your other state,
Where the world appears
Not as it appears here and now.

---

* Śivā is the feminine aspect of Śiva, that is, his *śakti*. Here she is personified as his consort Pārvatī, and represents the manifestation of the natural world (*prakṛti*).

The Seventeenth Song

•

A High Regard for Divine Amusements

Ah, most glorious   1
Is this blissful festival of worship
From which spring tears
Of the sweet nectar of immortality.

All actions connected with your worship   2
Will promote *siddhis*.
But for your devotees
Who are already one with you,
These actions are *siddhis* in and of themselves.

Those who in every state worship you always   3
As having assumed the form of all things—
They indeed
Are my chosen deities.

The *siddha** leaves behind the effort of meditation,   4
For all of his joy is obtained from your touch.
That, O Lord, for the devotees
Comprises an act of worship.

The time of the equinox,   5
Whose essence is equanimity,
Is celebrated by the devotees continuously:
For always does their worship consist
Of the sweet bliss of your devotion.

---

* A *siddha* (literally, "perfected one") is one who has attained the highest realization
of Śiva-consciousness.

Seventeenth Song

6   Without a beginning, without an end,
And unlimited by time—
This is the essence of worship, O Lord,
Performed only by devotees.

7   They are the lords
Even over Brahmā and the other gods,
And they are the recipients of auspiciousness—
Those in whom the festival of worship
Stays constant even while dreaming
And indeed even in dreamless sleep.

8   Devotees celebrate the festival of worship
Not only while performing *japa*,
Pouring oblations into the fire,
Bathing, or meditating—
But in all states.

9   Who among the leading gods—
Indra, Brahmā, and the others—
And even among ascetics,
Is equal to the one who enjoys
The sweet nectar of your worship?

10   In the great festival of your worship
The devotees attain the attainable:
The sole cause of the world's annihilation.
This they understand indeed.*

11   Resting in the brilliance of your consciousness,
May I ever worship you, O Lord,
By means of body, speech, and mind,
The products of the thirty-six *tattva*s.†

12   Contented, enjoying attachment to your worship,
May all of my time become endless.

---

* That is, ordinary people have insight neither into the worship of Śiva nor his true indentity.

† A *tattva* (literally, "thatness") is a category of manifestation. Kashmir Śaiva philosophies recognize thirty-six *tattva*s; Sāṃkhya, by comparison, admits twenty-five. For further discussion, see the introduction.

Only for this
Is it that I pray.

May my yearning for the enjoyment   13
Of the immortal bliss of your worship
Grow greater each day,
Ever yielding a bounteous harvest.

In your ocean brimming over   14
With the immortal bliss of unity
Cast outward at the dissolution of the universe,
May I there remain, O Great Soul, ever adoring you.

Having become pure and uncomplicated   15
By cutting through the knots of latent desires,
The devotees can finally dedicate their minds
To the sweet act of your worship.

Even while resting on their objects   16
The faculties of these senses provide
The devotees with the immortal wine
Essential to your worship, O Lord.

For devotees irresistably inflamed   17
With the burning heat of ardent devotion,
What other means of extinguishment* are needed
Than plunging into the nectar of your worship?

May I experience the endless joy, O Lord,   18
Of drinking the nectar of the worship of your feet:
The only means to receive your grace.

In every action, at all times   19
Let me enjoy the supreme bliss
Of intoxication from the immortal wine
Resulting from your worship, O Lord.

---

* The word used here for "extinguishment" is *nirvāṇa*, which is used, of course, in a technical sense to denote spiritual emancipation. Thus both the desire and the quenching are brought about by and are found in Śiva.

Seventeenth Song

20 To the devotees
    The meaning of the supreme endeavor of your worship
    Is quite obvious.
    They experience from it
    A joy beyond all expectation.

21 In my opinion,
    Not even a trace of the wealth of joy
    Is attained until one experiences
    The great festival of your worship.

22 Immersed in worship, the devotees find themselves
    Deep within your being
    Without effort, without concern
    For any accessories.

23 Nothing remains for them to achieve,
    Nothing is difficult for them to obtain:
    The devotees wander the earth without purpose,
    Drunk only with the joy of worshiping you.

24 Whose consciousness is expanded
    With intense devotion
    Has a unique, praiseworthy style of worship
    Unsullied by entreaties, O Granter of Boons.

25 What beauty, what delight,
    What other wealth,
    Or what other liberation
    Does not exist
    Where is worshiped the Transcendent Lord?

26 Nourished by the nectar
    Of pure devotion rippling within,
    Let my body become fit for your worship.

27 O Mighty One! Lord of the Worlds!
    Although my actions are uniquely unfettered,
    I would become unfettered
    If indeed it were required
    To enjoy your worship.

Those few who while meditating   28
Thirst for your vision and your touch
Receive the cool, sweet,
Deep lake of your worship.

Just as you   29
Are the only object of delightful worship
In this world, O Lord,
So also is the devotee
A deserving object of delightful worship.

O Master! How glorious   30
Is your great festival of worship,
Which reduces to ashes
Even the thirty-six *tattvas*.

Praised be those, O Lord,   31
Whose water of immortal devotion
Makes worthy of worship
Even the materials of your ceremony.

Having begun to meditate on you with a *mantra*,   32
Certain of your devotees, O Lord,
Even in their transcendental beings
Cannot contain their ecstacy.

Rejoicing as if they had been made kings,   33
Certain of your devotees in the festival of worship
Pour out the wine of immortality
Everywhere throughout the world.

Those chosen few whose pleasures entail   34
The endless imbibing of the nectar of your worship—
Are they gods, or liberated beings,
Or are they something else, O Lord?

Absorbing the universe into themselves   35
As the materials of worship,

How immeasurably heavy—and yet how light—
Become the devotees!*

36   For devotees, the agitation
Caused by the projection of the senses
When performing worship
Is indeed the source of immortality
Just as the agitation of the ocean of milk
Was for the gods.

37   Some consider worship as the wish-granting cow
That gratifies all desires,
But others, turning inward,
Drink a milk sweeter than streams of nectar.

38   Even the projection of senses
Known as this world
Fosters the initiation of the devotees
Into the supreme unearthly festival of worship.

39   In the heat of intense devotion, O Lord,
Worshiping you as my true self
Does not cause me to be plaintive;
It is, rather, the highest fruit of plaintiveness.

40   Some consider worship only as a means
Of striving for your state.
But for devotees
It is a process—
During which one enjoys
The sweet bliss of union with you.

41   Although unconventional, the worship
Of those who have become free
Through delirious devotion—
What a sublime end it reaches!

42   O Śambhu, you alone
Are the true, wondrous object of worship

---

* The powers of becoming infinitely heavy (*garimā*) and infinitely light (*laghimā*) are two of the eight *siddhi*s.

That emanates from hearts stunned
By tasting the sweet nectar of devotion.

Master, while engaging in your worship   43
Let my senses become full, pure, devoted,
And strong.

Immersed in your worship, O Lord,   44
The absolute treasure of all worship,
Oh, what unearthly splendor
Radiates from the senses.

Such humility   45
Is truly seen only in you,
O Master, who, even though lord of the universe,
Are worshiped by servants
And are obtained.

Whether out of the concrete or the abstract,   46
Out of existence or nonexistence,
May the great festival of your worship
Ever radiate in me,
Who have been made worthy of praise.

Adoration to those who, having offered up   47
All of their desires, anger, and pride,
Perform your worship incessantly.
With them are you truly pleased!

Most glorious   48
Is this path of worship through devotion,
Which, though performed with pieces of straw,
Is accomplished indeed with jewels.

The Eighteenth Song

•

Becoming Clear

1   O Lord of the Universe!
     Only your devotees, having discovered you
     From within the universe
     Again find the universe as within you,
     For nothing in the world is beyond their reach.

2   You dominate one state;
     Another is dominated by Bhavānī,*
     Pregnant with all of material creation.
     Ultimately, there is no difference
     Between Devī, the three worlds, and you.

3   People given to vanity
     Do not understand the essence of beauty,
     Or indeed that the essence of everything
     That exists is beautiful.
     Alas, the mind, although eager, even then
     Does not realize the essence of the self.
     Alas, I am lost!

4   I bow to him who, having made his dwelling
     In his own self, consisting of your essence,
     Abounds with the wealth of the worship of your feet
     Heedless of food, heedless of cover.

---

* Bhavānī is Śiva's consort in her mild, benevolent form as Pārvatī, or the mother of
the whole universe and all that exists.

This world, though dwelling comfortably 5
Within your body,
Is burning within.
Through your own will
Grant that here and now
I may be filled with the bliss of worshiping you.

With mind taken with drinking the nectar 6
Of worshiping spontaneously
The pair of your lotus feet,
Let me become a pilgrim of the world
Encountering in the accumulation of things
Only bliss.

With you, O Lord, shining clearly 7
In all worldly transactions,
Let all things appear to me
As constantly coming and going.

Let me forever wander about 8
Only within you,
Or as one with you.
Let there not be a moment
When I am not glorified as being one with you.

Rich with your worship, 9
Your devotees frolic
In this ocean of the world
Brimming with the cool nectar
That flows from your limbs.

In the vast forest of your worship, 10
O Lord, may I, your devotee,
Forever rest in the cool shade
Beneath the tree of Supreme Sound.

O Lord! Appear before me 11
Adorned with your three eyes
And trident
Just as to all beings

Eighteenth Song

You appear in all things
As light.

12   I have dedicated my ego to you
As an offering of devotion.
When will you be pleased enough
To become everywhere
The object of my sight?

13   Dwelling in the ocean of supreme bliss,
With mind absorbed only in your worship,
Let me engage in worldly affairs,
Relishing the ineffable at the same time.

14   All that is here in this world is yours.
Who could even begin to explain its essence?
Even so, your name, form, and movements
Captivate my heart,
O Captivator as you are!*

15   Those who are filled with devotion
Have not the slightest craving
For happiness as a means to attaining peace.
In the presence of the Heart-captivator,
They do not even remember to pray
For liberation.

16   Wakefulness, dreaming, or deep sleep—
Whatever the state—
When those who are worthy of devotion
Turn their attention toward you,
All this becomes a great festival.

17   The modifications of the senses,
Including the mind,
Have such an inconstant nature!
How does one

* Hara, an epithet of Śiva, denotes a variety of related meanings ranging from *Captivator* to *Raptor* to *Annihilator*, and so forth.

Who is radiant with the wealth of devotion
Make them become steady, firm, and wise, O Lord?

Nothing that you created is distinct from you,   18
And nothing that you created is other than bliss.
Yet all is sorrow and disharmony.
May you be glorified,
O Abode of unique bewilderment!

The impurity of differentiation   19
Having been washed away by the brimming nectar
Filling the abyss of obscuration,
And having trampled doubt, the invincible enemy,
Let me have your vision endlessly.

O Lord, inspire my whole being   20
So that I may be attached to you always,
And having come extremely close,
Let me worship you intently
In your true form.

No one at all is competent to praise you.   21
Who could ever begin to speak of your beauty?
But my prayer is always this—
That I may ever behold the Lord.

The Nineteenth Song

•

The Meaning Revealed

1   Beyond the range of prayer
Is the bestower of wondrous fruit,
The One of unparalleled behavior,
The wishing tree of heaven—
May Śiva be glorified!

2   Everything in the world is obtained from you,
The single source of the multitude of objects.
Still, to me you do not reveal
Your being as my own self—
It remains afar.

3   The reality behind everything
Is the conscious being
Who consists of the powers of knowledge and action,
The Great Lord.
Otherwise, not even a name would be possible,
Let alone anything else.

4   O Lord, set me on the path
That destroys dreadful suffering
And leads toward your recognition.
Let me as a result
Attain the state of merging with you.

5   When shall spiritual perfection
Bejewelled with the memory of your spotless feet
Come from you to me,
Causing awe in the hearts of perfected beings?

104

O Lord, when shall I behold   6
Your flawless countenance
Emitting floods of nectar
Drowning the whole world?

When, O Lord, shall your form,   7
Which appears only in a moment of recollection,
Fill with sublime nectar
The deep abysses that keep me from you?

Intent on the experience of your sublime nectar,   8
My mind still is not free of unsteadiness.
When will this happen, O Lord?
Oh, may it be soon!

Let me experience   9
All pairs of opposites
Not as dry and lacking the nectar
Of the bliss of your union,
But as dedicated to you.

O Lord! Let your spotless rays   10
Shine before me, face to face,
So that the darkness of physical and mental torments
Be completely dispelled.

O Celestial One, grant that I may overcome   11
The enemies along your path,
The sense-thieves
Who conceal the highest reality.

Soon, O Mighty One, fill my mind   12
With floods of the nectar of your devotion
So that these vain desires be completely submerged
And swept away.

Why is it, O Unborn One,   13
That your devotion does not shine
In the state of liberation
To one still bearing mortal characteristics?

Therefore raise me to a state of perfection
Befitting me as I am.

14 Let me not become proud, O Lord,
In the attainment of mere *siddhi*s.
For the radiance of *aṇimā* and the other powers,
And even of liberation itself,
Is but scant in the face of your devotion.

15 Just this much I pray:
That the Lord be pleased with me, his servant,
Who could never begin to understand
All that has been given
By the Lord of the Three Worlds.

16 In the lake of my mind, spilling over
With the bliss of the memory of your form,
May the lotuses of the pair of your feet
Ever bloom, effusing
Nectar most delicious and sublime.

17 This, the Lord, Tryambaka,
Is my father
And Bhavānī is my mother.
To me there is no second in the world.
With this realization
May I wander in the highest ecstacy.

The Twentieth Song

•

The Meaning Savored

I bow to the Master, Lord of the Three Worlds,　　　　　　1
White with ashes, three-eyed,
Bearing the serpent as sacred thread
And crescent moon as diadem.

Homage to the one wearing as raiment　　　　　　2
His own lustrous halo of radiant beams,
Bedecked with a glittering garland of skulls
For the festival of dance at the end of the world.

I bow to the eternally sacred abodes,　　　　　　3
Whose deity is Hara,
Whose activities are worthy of Hara,
And whose very breath of life is dedicated
Only to Hara.

Beyond your lordship is yet another　　　　　　4
One of your amusements—
That is, by sheer will I find
Spontaneous means to your glorious acts.

When the whole universe　　　　　　5
Honors just this much of your splendor—
The mere play in the world—
How infinite indeed
Must be your bliss!

How can one not be beatified　　　　　　6
Who is loved by Gauri's Hara?

Twentieth Song

And how can Hara not be
The supreme beloved of Gaurī?

7   Just as the roots of that sacred tree
Lie in sublime and everlasting recognition,
So too are formed its branches of sense perception.

8   When the itch for devotion flares up
Worship comes into being
As a great pillar of smearing-stone.

9   Glory to the Master,
Whose recreation is the act of creation,
Who delights in preservation,
And who rests contentedly,
Satisfied with the meal of the three worlds.

10   I bow to them, who,
Going nowhere and renouncing nothing,
Yet view all this as your glorious abode.

11   What else remains to be desired
By those rolling in the wealth of devotion?
For those deprived of it,
What else is worthy of desire?

12   Where even agonies transform into pleasure
And poison into nectar,
Where the world itself becomes liberation,
That is the path of Śaṅkara.

13   In the beginning, the middle, or the final stages,
There is no pain for your devotees, O Lord.
Still, we are suffering.
What is this? Tell me!

14   O Lord, some seek your realization
Through knowledge, through *yoga*,
Or through other disciplines.
But this realization shines forth constantly
Only to the self-willed devotees.

There is no plaintiveness for devotees   15
Nor any worry,
For their own self is identical with you.
Even then, in the external state
The indescribable word *O Śiva* is on their lips.

O Lord, I praise your Kriyā Śakti,   16
Light of all lights,
Filled with universal consciousness as
"I am all this."

O Celestial One, all beings,   17
Including Brahmā, Indra, and Viṣṇu,
View their objects as food.
Therefore, I glorify the universe
As consisting only of you.

Because being and nonbeing are relative,   18
Everything apart from me is unreal.
This alone is the significance
Of your play of dissolution, O Lord.

By mere recognition, O Granter of Boons,   19
Does your transcendental form emerge
Before those rolling in the wealth of devotion.
And thus do they conquer all causes of pain.

As though saturated with the wine   20
Of the nectar of devotion,
With vital organs radiating with delight,
The adventurous ones dance through the night
With Śiva's attendants, a party of ghosts.

With the same devotional mood   21
In which I began these hymns,
May I, O Śambhu, grow ever more secure.

oṃ

Sanskrit Text of the Śivastotrāvalī

The First Song

•

Bhaktivilāsākhyaṃ prathamaṃ stotram

oṃ

na dhyāyato na japataḥ syādyasyāvidhipūrvakam   1
evameva śivabhāsastaṃ numo bhaktiśālinam

ātmā mama bhavadbhaktisudhāpānayuvā'pi san   2
lokayātrārajorāgātpalitairiva dhūsaraḥ

labdhatatsaṃpadāṃ bhaktimatāṃ tvatpuravāsinām   3
saṃcāro lokamārge'pi syāttayaiva vijṛmbhayā

sākṣādbhavanmaye nātha sarvasmin bhuvanāntare   4
kiṃ na bhaktimatāṃ kṣetram mantraḥ kvaiṣām na siddhyati

jayanti bhaktipīyūṣarasāsavavaronmadāḥ   5
advitīyā api sadā tvaddvitīyā api prabho

anantānandasindhoste nātha tattvaṃ vidanti te   6
tādṛśa eva ye sāndrabhaktyānandarasāplutāḥ

tvamevātmeśa sarvasya sarvaścātmani rāgavān   7
iti svabhāvasiddhāṃs tvadbhaktiṃ jānañjayejjanaḥ

nātha vedyakṣaye kena na dṛśyo'syekakaḥ sthitaḥ   8
vedyavedakasaṃkṣobhe'pyasi bhaktaiḥ sudarśanaḥ

anantānandasarasī devī priyatamā yathā   9
aviyuktāsti te tadvadekā tvadbhaktirastu me

First Song

10   sarva eva bhavallābhaheturbhaktimatāṃ vibho
samvinmārgo'yamāhlādaduḥkhamohaistridhā sthitaḥ

11   bhavadbhaktyamṛtāsvādādbodhasya syātparāpi yā
daśā sā māṃ prati svāminnāsavasyeva śuktatā

12   bhavadbhaktimahāvidyā yeṣāmabhyāsamāgatā
vidyāvidyobhayasyāpi tā ete tattvavedinaḥ

13   āmulādvāglatā seyaṃ kramavisphāraśālinī
tvadbhaktisudhayā siktā tadrasāḍhyaphalāstu me

14   śivo bhūtvā yajeteti bhakto bhūtveti kathyate
tvameva hi vapuḥ sāraṃ bhaktairadvayaśodhitam

15   bhaktānāṃ bhavadadvaitasiddhyai kā nopapattayaḥ
tadasiddhyai nikṛṣṭānāṃ kāni nāvaraṇāni vā

16   kadācitkvāpi labhyo'si yogenetīśa vañcanā
anyathā sarvakakṣyāsu bhāsi bhaktimatāṃ katham

17   pratyāhārādyasaṃspṛṣṭo viśeṣo'sti mahānayam
yogibhyo bhaktibhājām yadvyutthāne'pi samāhitāḥ

18   na yogo na tapo nārcākramaḥ ko'pi pranīyate
amāye śivamārge'smin bhaktirekā praśasyate

19   sarvato vilasadbhaktitejodhvastāvṛtermama
pratyakṣasarvabhāvasya cintānāmapi naśyatu

20   śiva ityekaśabdasya jihvāgre tiṣṭhataḥ sadā
samastaviṣayāsvādo bhakteṣvevāsti ko'pyaho

21   śāntakallolaśītacchasvādubhaktisudhāmbudhau
alaukikarasāsvāde susthaiḥ ko'nāma gaṇyate

22   sādṛśaiḥ kiṃ na carvyeta bhavadbhaktimahauṣadhiḥ
tādṛśī bhagavanyasyā mokṣākhyo'nantaro rasaḥ

23   tā eva paramarthyante sampadaḥ sadbhirīśa yāḥ
tvadbhaktirasasambhogavisrambhaparipoṣikāḥ

112

bhavadbhaktisudhāsārastaiḥ kimapyupalakṣitaḥ   24
ye na rāgādi paṅke'smiṃllipyante patitā api

aṇimādiṣu mokṣānteṣvaṅgeṣveva phalābhidhā   25
bhavadbhaktervipakvāyā latāyā iva keṣucit

citraṃ nisargato nātha duḥkhabījamidaṃ manaḥ   26
tvadbhaktirasasaṃsiktam niḥśreyasamahāphalam

The Second Song

•

Sarvātmaparibhāvanākhyaṃ dvitīyaṃ stotram

1   agnīṣomaravibrahmaviṣṇusthāvarajaṅgama
    svarūpa bahurūpāya namaḥ saṃvinmayāya te

2   viśvendhanamahākṣārānulepaśucivarcase
    mahānalāya bhavate viśvaikahaviṣe namaḥ

3   paramāmṛtasāndrāya śītalāya śivāgnaye
    kasmaicidviśvasaṃploṣaviṣamāya namo'stu te

4   mahādevāya rudrāya śaṅkarāya śivāya te
    maheśvarāyāpi namaḥ kasmaicinmantramūrtaye

5   namo nikṛttaniḥśoṣatrailokyavigaladvasā-
    vasekaviṣamāyāpi maṅgalāya śivāgnaye

6   samastalakṣaṇāyoga eva yasyopalakṣaṇam
    tasmai namo'stu devāya kasmaicidapi śambhave

7   vedāgamaviruddhāya vedāgamavidhāyine
    vedāgamatattvāya guhyāya svāmine namaḥ

8   saṃsāraikanimittāya saṃsāraikavirodhine
    namaḥ samsārarūpāya niḥsaṃsārāya śambhave

9   mūlāya madhyāyāgrāya mūlamadhyāgramūrtaye
    kṣīnāgramadhyamūlāya namaḥ pūrṇāya śambhave

114

namaḥ sukṛtasaṃbharavipākaḥ sakṛdapyasau   10
yasya nāmagrahaḥ tasmai durlabhāya śivāya te

namaścarācarākāraparetanicayaiḥ sadā   11
krīḍate tubhyamekasmai cinmayāya kapāline

māyāvine viśuddhāya guhyāya prakaṭātmane   12
sūkṣmāya viśvarūpāya namaścitrāya śambhave

brahmendraviṣṇunirvyūḍhajagatsaṃhārakelaye   13
āścaryakaraṇīyāya namaste sarvaśaktaye

taṭeṣveva paribhrāntaiḥ labdhāstāstā vibhūtayaḥ   14
yasya tasmai namastubhyamagādhaharasindhave

māyāmayajagatsāndrapaṅkamadhyādhivāsine   15
alepāya namaḥ śambhuśatapatrāya śobhine

maṅgalāya pavitrāya nidhaye bhūṣaṇātmane   16
priyāya paramārthāya sarvotkṛṣṭāya te namaḥ

namaḥ satatabaddhāya nityanirmuktibhāgine   17
bandhamokṣavihīnāya kasmaicidapi śambhave

upahāsaikasāre'sminnetāvati jagattraye   18
tubhyamevādvitīyāya namo nityasukhāsine

dakṣiṇācārasārāya vāmācārābhilāṣiṇe   19
sarvācārāya śarvāya nirācārāya te namaḥ

yathā tathāpi yaḥ pūjyo yatratatrāpi yo'rcitaḥ   20
yo'pi vā so'pi vā yo'sau devastasmai namo'stu te

mumukṣujanasevyāya sarvasantāpahāriṇe   21
namo vitatalāvaṇyavarāya varadāya te

sadā nirantarānandarasanirbharitākhila-   22
trilokāya namastubhyaṃ svāmine nityaparvaṇe

sukhapradhānasaṃvedyasambhogairbhajate ca yat   23
tvāmeva tasmai ghorāya śaktivṛndāya te namaḥ

Second Song

24 munīnāmapyavijñeyaṃ bhaktisambandhaceṣṭitāḥ
    āliṅgantyapi yaṃ tasmai kasmaicidbhavate namaḥ

25 paramāmṛtakośāya paramāmṛtarāśaye
    sarvapāramyapāramyaprāpyāya bhavate namaḥ

26 mahāmantramayaṃ naumi rūpaṃ te svacchaśītalam
    apūrvamodasubhagaṃ parāmṛtarasolvaṇam

27 svātantryāmṛtapūrṇatvadaikyakhyātimahāpaṭe
    citraṃ nāstyeva yatreśa tannaumi tava śāsanam

28 sarvāśaṅkāsaniṃ sarvālakṣmīkālānalaṃ tathā
    sarvāmaṅgalyakalpāntaṃ mārgaṃ māheśvaraṃ numaḥ

29 jaya deva namo namo'stu te sakalaṃ viśvamidaṃ tavāśritam
    jagatāṃ parameśvaro bhavān paramekaḥ śaraṇāgato'smi te

116

The Third Song

•

Praṇayaprasādākhyaṃ tṛtīyaṃ stotram

sadasattvena bhāvānāṃ yuktā yā dvitayī gatiḥ   1
tāmullaṅghya tṛtīyasmai namaścitrāya śambhave

āsurarṣijanādasminnasvatantre jagattraye   2
svatantrāste svatantrasya ye tavaivānujīvinaḥ

aśeṣaviśvakhacitabhavadvapuranusmṛtiḥ   3
yeṣāṃ bhavarujāmekaṃ bheṣajaṃ te sukhāsinaḥ

sitātapatraṃ yasyenduḥ svaprabhāparipūritaḥ   4
cāmaraṃ svardhunīsrotaḥ sa ekaḥ parameśvaraḥ

prakāśāṃ śītalāmekāṃ śuddhāṃ śaśikalāmiva   5
dṛśaṃ vitara me nātha kāmapyamṛtavāhinīm

tvaccidānandajaladheścyutāḥ saṃvittivipruṣaḥ   6
imāḥ kathaṃ me bhagavannāmṛtāsvādasundarāḥ

tvayi rāgarase nātha na magnaṃ hṛdayaṃ prabho   7
yeṣāmahṛdayā eva te'vajñāspadamīdṛśāḥ

prabhuṇā bhavatā yasya jātaṃ hṛdayamelanam   8
prābhavīṇāṃ vibhūtīnāṃ paramekaḥ sa bhājanam

harṣāṇāmatha śokānāṃ sarveṣāṃ plāvakaḥ samam   9
bhavaddhyānāmṛtāpūro nimnāṇimnabhuvāmiva

keva na syādṛśā teṣāṃ sukhasambhāranirbharā   10
yeṣāmātmādhikeneśa na kvāpi virahastvayā

Third Song

11   garjāmi bata nṛtyāmi pūrṇā mama manorathāḥ
      svāmī mamaiṣa ghaṭito yattvamatyantarocanaḥ

12   nānyadvedyaṃ kriyā yatra nānyo yogo vidā ca yat
      jñānaṃ syāt kintu viśvaikapūrṇā cittvaṃ vijṛmbhate

13   durjayānāmanantānām duḥkhānāṃ sahasaiva te
      hastātpalāyitā yeṣāṃ vāci śaśvacchivadhvaniḥ

14   uttamaḥ puruṣo'nyo'sti yuṣmaccheṣaviśeṣitaḥ
      tvaṃ mahāpuruṣastveko niḥśeṣapuruṣāśrayaḥ

15   jayanti te jagadvandyā dāsāste jagatāṃ vibho
      saṃsārārṇava evaiṣa yeṣāṃ krīḍāmahāsaraḥ

16   āsatāṃ tāvadanyāni dainyānīha bhavajjuṣām
      tvameva prakaṭībhūyā ityanenaiva lajjyate

17   matparaṃ nāsti tatrāpi jāpako'smi tadaikyataḥ
      tattvena japa ityakṣamālayā diśasi kvacit

18   sato'vaśyaṃ paramasatsacca tasmātparaṃ prabho
      tvaṃ cāsatassataścānyastenāsi sadasanmayaḥ

19   sahasrasūryakiraṇādhikaśuddhaprakāśavān
      api tvaṃ sarvabhuvanavyāpako'pi na dṛśyase

20   jaḍe jagati cidrūpaḥ kila vedye'pi vedakaḥ
      vibhurmite ca yenāsi tena sarvottamo bhavān

21   alamākranditairanyairiyadeva puraḥ prabhoḥ
      tīvraṃ viraumi yannātha muhyāmyevaṃ vidannapi

The Fourth Song

•

Surasodbalākhyāṃ caturthaṃ stotram

capalam asi yadapi mānasa 1
tatrāpi ślāghyase yato bhajase
śaraṇānāmapi śaraṇaṃ
tribhuvanagurumambikākāntam

ullaṅghya vividhadaivata- 2
sopānakramamupeyaśivacaraṇān
āśrityāpyadharatarāṃ bhūmiṃ
nādyāpi citramujjhāmi

prakaṭaya nijamadhvānaṃ 3
sthagayatarāmakhilalokacaritāni
yāvadbhavāmi bhagavaṃ-
stava sapadi sadodito dāsaḥ

śiva śiva śambho śaṅkara 4
śaraṇāgatavatsalāśu kuru karuṇām
tava caraṇakamalayugala-
smaraṇaparasya hi sampado'dūre

tāvakāṅghrikamalāsanalīnā 5
ye yathāruci jagadracayanti
te viriñcimadhikāramalenā-
liptamasvavaśamīśa hasanti

tvatprakāśavapuṣo na vibhinnaṃ 6
kiṃcana prabhavati pratibhātum
tatsadaiva bhagavan parilabdho-
'sīśvara prakṛtito'pi vidūraḥ

Fourth Song

7   pādapaṅkajarasaṃ tava kecid
      bhedaparyuṣitavṛttimupetāḥ
      kecanāpi rasayanti tu sadhyo
      bhātamakṣatavapurdvayaśūnyam

8   nātha vidyudiva bhāti vibhāte
      yā kadācana mamāmṛtadigdhā
      sā yadi sthirataraiva bhavettat
      pūjito'si vidhivatkimutānyat

9   sarvamasyaparamasti na kiṃcid
      vastvavastu yadi veti mahatyā
      prajñāya vyavasito'tra yathaiva
      tvaṃ tathaiva bhava suprakaṭo me

10   svecchayaiva bhagavannijamārge
      kāritaḥ padamahaṃ prabhunaiva
      tatkathaṃ janavadeva carāmi
      tvatpadocitamavaimi na kiṃcit

11   ko'pi deva hṛdi teṣu tāvako
      jṛmbhate subhagabhāva uttamaḥ
      tvatkathāmbudaninādacātakā
      yena te'pi subhagīkṛtāściram

12   tvajjuṣāṃ tvayi kayāpi līlayā
      rāga eṣa paripoṣamāgataḥ
      yadviyogabhuvi saṅkathā tathā
      saṃsmṛtiḥ phalati saṃgamotsavam

13, 14 yo vicitrarasasekavardhitaḥ
      śaṅkareti śataśo'pyudīritaḥ
      śabda āviśati tiryagāśaye-
      ṣvapyayaṃ navanavaprayojanaḥ
      te jayanti mukhamaṇḍale bhraman
      asti yeṣu niyataṃ śivadhvaniḥ
      yaḥ śāśīva prasṛto'mṛtāśayāt
      svādu saṃsravati cāmṛtaṃ param*

* Most manuscripts place these two verses together with one long commentary
following both. Cf. also 10.5, 6 and 10.18, 19.

parisamāptamivogramidaṃ jagad 15
vigalito'viralo manaso malaḥ
tadapi nāsti bhavatpurā-
rgalakavāṭavighaṭṭanamaṇvapi

satataphullabhavanmukhapaṅkajo- 16
daravilokanalālasacetasaḥ
kimapi tatkuru nātha manāgiva
sphurasi yena mamābhimukhasthitiḥ

tvadavibhedamateraparaṃ nu kiṃ 17
sukhamihāsti vibhūtirathāparā
tadiha tāvakadāsajanasya kiṃ
kupathameti manaḥ parihṛtya tām

kṣaṇamapīha na tāvakadāsatāṃ 18
prati bhaveyamahaṃ kila bhājanam
bhavadabhedarasāsavamādarā-
davirataṃ rasayeyamahaṃ na cet

na kila paśyati satyamayaṃ jana- 19
stava vapur dvayadṛṣṭimalīmasaḥ
tadapi sarvavidāśritavatsalaḥ
kimidamāraṭitaṃ na śṛṇoṣi me

smarasi nātha kadācidapīhitaṃ 20
viṣayasaukhyamathāpi mayārthitam
satatameva bhavadvapurīkṣaṇā-
mṛtamabhīṣṭamalaṃ mama dehi tat

kila yadaiva śivādhvani tāvake 21
kṛtapado'smi maheśa tavecchayā
śubhaśatānyuditāni tadaiva me
kimaparaṃ mṛgaye bhavataḥ prabho

yatra so'stamayameti vivasvāṃ- 22
ścandramaḥ prabhṛtibhiḥ saha sarvaiḥ
kāpi sā vijayate śivarātriḥ
svaprabhāprasarabhāsvararūpā

Fourth Song

23 apyupārjitamahaṃ triṣu loke-
    ṣvadhipatyamamareśvara manye
    nīrasaṃ tadakhilaṃ bhavadaṅghri-
    sparśanāmṛtarasena vihīnam

24 bata nātha dṛḍho'yam ātmabandho
    bhavadakhyātimayastvayaiva kḷptaḥ
    yadayaṃ prathamānameva me tvā-
    mavadhīrya ślathate na leśato'pi

25 mahatāmamareśa pūjyamāno-
    'pyaniśaṃ tiṣṭhasi pūjakaikarūpaḥ
    bahirantarapīha dṛśyamānaḥ
    sphurasi draṣṭṛśarīra eva śaśvat

The Fifth Song

•

Svabalanideśanākhyaṃ
pañcamaṃ stotram

tvatpādapadmasamparkamātrasambhogasaṅginam   1
galepādikayā nātha māṃ svaveśma praveśaya

bhavatpādāmbujarajorājirañjitamūrdhajaḥ   2
apārarabhasārabdhanartanaḥ syāmahaṃ kadā

tvadekanātho bhagavanniyadevārthaye sadā   3
tvadantarvasatirmūko bhaveyaṃ mānyathā budhaḥ

aho sudhānidhe svāminn aho mṛṣṭa trilocana   4
aho svādo virūpakṣetyeva nṛtyeyamāraṭan

tvapādapadmasaṃsparśaparimīlitalocanaḥ   5
vijṛmbheya bhavadbhaktimadirāmadaghūrṇitaḥ

cittabhūbhṛdbhuvi vibho vaseyaṃ kvāpi yatra sā   6
nirantaratvatpralāpamayī vṛttirmahārasā

yatra devīsametastvamāsaudhādā ca gopurāt   7
bahurūpaḥ sthitastasminvāstavyaḥ syāmahaṃ pure

samullasantu bhagavan bhavadbhānumarīcayaḥ   8
vikasatveṣa yāvanme hṛtpadmaḥ pūjanāya te

prasīda bhagavan yena tvatpade patitaṃ sadā   9
mano me tattadāsvādya kṣīvediva galediva

123

Fifth Song

10 praharṣādvātha śokādvā yadi kuṅyāddhaṭādapi
    bāhyādathāntarādbhāvātprakaṭībhava me prabho

11 bahirapyantarapi tatsyandamānaṃ sadāstu me
    bhavatpādāmbujasparśāmṛtamatyantaśītalam

12 tvatpādasaṃsparśasudhāsaraso'ntarnimajjanam
    ko'pyeṣa sarvasambhogalaṅghī bhogo'stu me sadā

13 niveditamupādatsva rāgādi bhagavanmayā
    ādāya cāmṛtīkṛtya bhuṅkṣva bhaktajanaiḥ samam

14 aśeṣabhuvanāhāranityatṛptaḥ sukhāsanam
    svāmin gṛhāṇa dāseṣu prasādālokanakṣaṇam

15 antarbhakticamatkāracarvaṇāmīlitekṣaṇaḥ
    namo mahyaṃ śivāyeti pūjayam syāṃ tṛṇānyapi

16 api labdhabhavadbhāvaḥ svātmollāsamayaṃ jagat
    paśyan bhaktirasābhogairbhaveyamaviyojitaḥ

17 ākāmkṣaṇīyamaparaṃ yena nātha na vidyate
    tava tenādvitīyasya yuktaṃ yatparipūrṇatā

18 hasyate nṛtyate yatra rāgadveṣādi bhujyate
    pīyate bhaktipīyūṣarasastatprāpnuyāṃ padam

19 tat tadapūrvāmoda-
        tvaccintākusumavāsanā dṛḍhatām
    etu mama manasi yāvan-
        naśyatu durvāsanāgandhaḥ

20 kva nu rāgādiṣu rāgaḥ
        kva ca haracaraṇāmbujeṣu rāgitvam
    itthaṃ virodharasikaṃ
        bodhaya hitamamara me hṛdayam

21 vicaranyogadaśāsvapi
        viṣayavyāvṛttivartamāno'pi
    tvaccintāmadirāmada-
        taralīkṛtahṛdaya eva syām

124

vāci manomatiṣu tathā 22
śarīraceṣṭāsu karaṇaracitāsu
sarvatra sarvadā me
puraḥsaro bhavatu bhaktirasaḥ

śivaśivaśiveti nāmani 23
tava niravadhi nātha japyamāne'smin
āsvādayan bhaveyaṃ
kamapi mahārasamapunaruktam

sphuradanantacidātmakaviṣṭape 24
parinipītasamastajaḍādhvani
agaṇitāparacinmayagaṇḍike
pravicareyamahaṃ bhavato'rcitā

svavapuṣi sphuṭabhāsini śāśvate 25
sthitikṛte na kimapyupayujyate
iti matiḥ sudṛḍhā bhavatāt paraṃ
mama bhavaccaraṇābjarajaḥ śuceḥ

kimapi nātha kadācana cetasi 26
sphurati tadbhavadaṃghritalaspṛśām
galati yatra samastamidaṃ sudhā-
sarasi viśvamidaṃ diśa me sadā

The Sixth Song

•

Adhvavisphuraṇākhyaṃ ṣaṣṭhaṃ stotram

1 kṣaṇamātramapīśāna viyuktasya tvayā mama
nibiḍaṃ tapyamānasya sadā bhūyā dṛśaḥ padam

2 viyogasāre saṃsāre priyeṇa prabhuṇā tvayā
aviyuktaḥ sadaiva syāṃ jagatāpi viyojitaḥ

3 kāyavāṅmanasairyatra yāmi sarvaṃ tvameva tat
ityeṣa paramārtho'pi paripūrṇo'stu me sadā

4 nirvikalpo mahānandapūrṇo yadvadbhavāṃstathā
bhavatstutikarī bhūyādanurūpaiva vāṅmama

5 bhavadāveśataḥ paśyan bhāvaṃ bhāvaṃ bhavanmayam
vicareyaṃ nirākāṅkṣaḥ praharṣaparipūritaḥ

6 bhagavanbhavataḥ pūrṇam paśyeyamakhilaṃ jagat
tāvataivāsmi santuṣṭastato na parikhidyase

7 vilīyamānāstvayyeva vyomni meghalavā iva
bhāvā vibhāntu me śaśvatkramanairmalyagāminaḥ

8 svaprabhāprasaradhvastāparyantadhvāntasantatiḥ
santataṃ bhātu me ko'pi bhavamadhyādbhavanmaṇiḥ

9 kāṃ bhūmikāṃ nādhiśeṣe kiṃ tatsyādyanna te vapuḥ
śrāntastenāprayāsena sarvatastvāmavāpnuyām

126

bhavadaṅgapariṣvaṅgasambhogaḥ svecchayaiva me   10
ghaṭatāmiyati prāpte kiṃ nātha na jitaṃ mayā

prakaṭībhava nānyābhiḥ prārthanābhiḥ kadarthanāḥ   11
kurmaste nātha tāmyantastvāmeva mṛgayāmahe

The Seventh Song

•

Vidhuravijayanāmadheyaṃ saptamaṃ stotram

1   tvayyānandasarasvati
     samarasatāmetya nātha mama cetaḥ
     pariharatu sakṛdiyantaṃ
     bhedādhīnaṃ mahānartham

2   etanmama na tvidamiti
     rāgadveṣādinigaḍadṛḍhamūle
     nātha bhavanmayataikya-
     pratyayaparaśuḥ patatvantaḥ

3   galatu vikalpakalaṅkāvalī
     samullasatu hṛdi nirargalatā
     bhagavannānandarasa-
     plutāstu me cinmayī mūrtiḥ

4   rāgādimayabhavāṇḍaka-
     luṭhitaṃ tvadbhaktibhāvanāmbikā taistaiḥ
     āpyāyayatu rasairmāṃ
     pravṛddhapakṣo yathā bhavāmi khagaḥ

5   tvaccaraṇabhāvanāmṛta-
     rasasārāsvādanaipuṇaṃ labhatām
     cittamidaṃ niḥśeṣita-
     viṣayaviṣāsaṅgavāsanāvadhi me

6   tvadbhaktitapanadīdhiti-
     saṃsparśavaśānmamaiṣa dūrataram

cetomaṇirvimūñcatu
rāgādikataptavahnikaṇān

tasminpade bhavantaṃ   7
satatamupaślokayeyamatyuccaiḥ
hariharyaśvaviriñcā
api yatra bahiḥ pratīkṣante

bhaktimadajanitavibhrama-   8
vaśena paśyeyamavikalaṃ karaṇaiḥ
śivamayamakhilaṃ lokaṃ
kriyāśca pūjāmayī sakalāḥ

māmakamanogṛhīta-   9
tvadbhaktikulāṅganāṇimādisutān
sūtvā subaddhamūlā
mameti buddhiṃ dṛḍhikurutām

The Eighth Song

•

Alaukikodbalanākhyam-
aṣṭamaṃ stotram

1 yaḥ prasādalava īśvarasthito
   yā ca bhaktiriva māmupeyuṣī
   tau parasparasamanvitau kadā
   tādṛśe vapuṣi rūḍhimeṣyataḥ

2 tvatprabhutvaparicarvaṇajanmā
   ko'pyudetu paritoṣaraso'ntaḥ
   sarvakālamiha me paramastu
   jñānayogamahimādi vidūre

3 lokavadbhavatu me viṣayeṣu
   sphīta eva bhagavanparitarṣaḥ
   kevalaṃ tava śarīratayaitān
   lokayeyamahamastavikalpaḥ

4 dehabhūmiṣu tathā manasi tvaṃ
   prāṇavartmani ca bhedamupete
   saṃvidaḥ pathiṣu teṣu ca tena
   svātmanā mama bhava sphuṭarūpaḥ

5 nijanijeṣu padeṣu patantvimāḥ
   karaṇavṛttaya ullasitā mama
   kṣaṇamapīśa manāgapi maiva bhūt
   tvadavibhedarasakṣatisāhasam

6 laghumasṛṇasitācchaśītalaṃ
   bhavadāveśavaśena bhāvayan

vapurakhilapadārthapaddhate-
rvyavahārānativartayeya tān

vikasatu svavapurbhavadātmakaṃ   7
  samupayāntu jaganti mamāṅgatām
vrajatu sarvamidaṃ dvayavalgitaṃ
  smṛtipathopagame'pyanupākhyatām

samudiyādapi tādṛśatāvakā-   8
nanavilokaparāmṛtasamplavaḥ
mama ghaṭeta yathā bhavadadvayā-
prathanaghoradarīparipūraṇam

api kadācana tāvakasaṅgamā-   9
mṛtakaṇācchuraṇena tanīyasā
sakalalokasukheṣu parāṅmukho
na bhavitāsmyubhayacyuta eva kim

satatameva bhavaccaraṇāmbujā-   10
karacarasya hi haṃsavarasya me
upari mūlatalād api cāntarā-
dupanamatvaja bhaktimṛṇālikā

upayāntu vibho samastavastūnyapi   '1
cintāviṣayaṃ dṛśaḥ padaṃ ca
mama darśanacintanaprakāśā-
mṛtasārāṇi paraṃ parisphurantu

parameśvara teṣu teṣu kṛcchre-   12
ṣvapi nāmopanamatsvahaṃ bhaveyam
na paraṃ gatabhīstvadaṅgasaṅgā-
dupajātādhikasammado'pi yāvat

bhavadātmani viśvamumbhitaṃ yad   13
bhavataivāpi bahiḥ prakāśyate tat
iti yaddṛḍhaniścayopajuṣṭaṃ
tadidānīṃ sphuṭameva bhāsatām

The Ninth Song

•

Svātantryavijayākhyaṃ navamaṃ stotram

1   kadā navarasārdrārdra-
    sambhogāsvādanotsukam
    pravarteta vihāyānyan
    mama tvatsparśane manaḥ

2   tvadekaraktastvatpāda-
    pūjāmātramahādhanaḥ
    kadā sākṣātkariṣyāmi
    bhavantamayamutsukaḥ

3   gāḍhānurāgavaśato
    nirapekṣībhūtamānaso'smi kadā
    paṭapaṭiti vighaṭitākhila-
    mahārgalastvāmupaiṣyāmi

4   svasaṃvitsārahṛdayā-
    dhiṣṭhānāḥ sarvadevatāḥ
    kadā nātha vaśīkuryāṃ
    bhavadbhaktiprabhāvataḥ

5   kadā me syādvibho bhūri
    bhaktyānandarasotsavaḥ
    yadālokasukhānandī
    pṛthaṅnāmāpi lapsyate

6   īśvaramabhayamudāraṃ
    pūrṇamakāraṇamapahnutātmānaṃ

sahasābhijñāya kadā
svāmijanaṃ lajjayiṣyāmi

kadā kāmapi tāṃ nātha 7
tava vallabhatāmiyām
yayā māṃ prati na kvāpi
yuktaṃ te syātpalāyitum

tattvato'śeṣajantūnāṃ 8
bhavatpūjāmayātmanām
dṛṣṭyānumoditarasā-
plāvitaḥ syāṃ kadā vibho

jñānasya paramā bhūmi- 9
ryogasya paramā daśā
tvadbhaktiryā vibho karhi
pūrṇa me syāttadarthitā

sahasaivasādya kadā 10
gāḍhamavaṣṭabhya harṣavivaśo'ham
tvaccaraṇavaranidhānaṃ
sarvasya prakaṭayiṣyāmi

paritaḥ prasaracchuddha- 11
tvadālokamayaḥ kadā
syāṃ yatheśa na kiñcinme
māyācchāyābilaṃ bhavet

ātmasātkṛtaniḥśeṣa- 12
maṇḍalo nirvyapekṣakaḥ
kadā bhaveyaṃ bhagavaṃ-
stvadbhaktagaṇanāyakaḥ

nātha lokābhimānānā- 13
mapūrvaṃ tvaṃ nibandhanam
mahābhimānaḥ karhi syāṃ
tvadbhaktirasapūritaḥ

aśeṣaviṣayāśūnya- 14
śrīsamāśleṣasusthitaḥ

śayīyamiva śītāṅghri-
kuśeśayayuge kadā

15 bhaktyāsavasamṛddhāyā-
stvatpūjābhogasampadaḥ
kadā pāraṃ gamiṣyāmi
bhaviṣyāmi kadā kṛtī

16 ānandabāṣpapūra-
skhalitaparibhrāntagadgadākrandaḥ
hāsollāsitavadana-
stvatsparśarasaṃ kadāpsyāmi

17 paśujanasamānavṛttā-
mavadhūya daśāmimāṃ kadā śambho
āsvādayeya tāvaka-
bhaktocitamātmano rūpam

18 labdhāṇimādisiddhi-
rvigalitasakalopatāpasantrāsaḥ
tvadbhaktirasāyanapāna-
kriḍhāniṣṭaḥ kadāsīya

19 nātha kadā sa tathāvidha
ākrando me samuccared vāci
yat samanantarameva
sphurati purastāvakī mūrtiḥ

20 gāḍhagāḍhabhavadaṅghrisarojā
liṅganavyasanatatparacetāḥ
vastvavastvidamayatnata eva
tvāṃ kadā samavalokayitāsmi

The Tenth Song

•

Avicchedabhaṅgākhyaṃ daśamaṃ stotram

na soḍhavyamavaśyam te jagadekaprabhoridam   1
māheśvarāśca lokānāmitareṣāṃ samāśca yat

ye sadaivānurāgeṇa bhavatpādānugāminaḥ   2
yatra tatra gatā bhogāṃste kāṃścid upabhuñjate

bhartā kālāntako yatra bhavāṃstatra kuto rujaḥ   3
tatra cetarabhogāśā kā lakṣmīryatra tāvakī

kṣanamātrasukhenāpi vibhuryenāsi labhyase   4
tadaiva sarvaḥ kālo'sya tvadānandena pūryate

ānandarasabinduste candramā galito bhuvi   5,6
sūryastathā te prasṛtaḥ saṃhārī tejasaḥ kaṇaḥ
baliṃ yāmastṛtīyāya netrāyāsmai tava prabho
alaukikasya kasyāpi māhātmyasyaikalakṣmaṇe

tenaiva dṛṣṭo'si bhavaddarśanādyo'tihṛṣyati   7
kathañcidyasya vā harṣaḥ ko'pi tena tvamīkṣitaḥ

yeṣāṃ prasanno'si vibho yairlabdhaṃ hṛdayaṃ tava   8
ākṛṣya tvatpurāttaistu bāhyamābhyantarīkṛtam

tvadṛte nikhilaṃ viśvaṃ samadṛgyātamīkṣyatām   9
īśvaraḥ punaretasya tvameko viṣamekṣaṇaḥ

10   āstāṃ bhavatprabhāveṇa vinā sattaiva nāsti yat
       tvaddūṣaṇakathā yeṣāṃ tvadṛte nopapadyate

11   bāhyāntarāntarāyālīkevale cetasi sthitiḥ
       tvayi cetsyānmama vibho kimanyadupayujyate

12   anye bhramanti bhagavannātmanyevātiduḥsthitāḥ
       anye bhramanti bhagavannātmanyevātisusthitāḥ

13   apītvapi bhavadbhaktisudhāmanavalokya ca
       tvāmīśa tvatsamācāramātrātsiddhyanti jantavaḥ

14   bhṛtyā vayaṃ tava vibho tena trijagatāṃ yathā
       bibharṣyātmānamevaṃ te bharttavyā vayamapyalam

15   parānandāmṛtamaye dṛṣṭo'pi jagadātmani
       tvayi sparśarase'tyantatarasutkaṇṭhito'smi te

16   deva duḥkhānyaśeṣāṇi yāni saṃsāriṇāmapi
       ghṛtyākhyabhavadīyātmayutānyāyānti sahyatām

17   sarvajñe sarvaśaktau ca tvayyeva sati cinmaye
       sarvathāpyasato nātha yuktāsya jagataḥ prathā

18,19 tvatprāṇitāḥ sphurantīme guṇā loṣṭopamā api
       nṛtyanti pavanoddhūtāḥ kārpāsāḥpicavo yathā
       yadi nātha guṇeṣvātmābhimāno na bhavettataḥ
       kena hīyeta jagatastvadekātmatayā prathā

20   vandyāste'pi mahīyāṃsaḥ pralayopagatā api
       tvatkopapāvakasparśapūtā ye parameśvara

21   mahāprakāśavapuṣi vispaṣṭe bhavati sthite
       sarvato'pīśa tatkasmāttamasi prasarāmyaham

22   avibhāgo bhavāneva svarūpamamṛtaṃ mama
       tathāpi martyadharmāṇāmahamevaikamāspadam

23   maheśvareti yasyāsti nāmakaṃ vāgvibhūṣaṇam
       praṇāmāṅkaśca śirasa sa evaikaḥ prabhāvitaḥ

sadasacca bhavāneva yena tenāprayāsataḥ 24
svarasenaiva bhagavaṃstathā siddhiḥ kathaṃ na me

śivadāsaḥ śivaikātmā kiṃ yannāsādayetsukham 25
tarpyo'smi devamukhyānāmapi yenāmṛtāsavaiḥ

hṛnnābhyorantarālasthaḥ prāṇināṃ pittavigrahaḥ 26
grasase tvaṃ mahāvahniḥ sarvaṃ sthāvarajaṅgamam

The Eleventh Song

•

Autsukyaviśvasitanāmaikādaśaṃ stotram

1 jagadidamatha vā suhṛdo
   bandhujano vā na bhavati mama kimapi
   tvaṃ punaretatsarvaṃ
   yadā tadā ko'paro me'stu

2 svāminmaheśvarastvaṃ
   sākṣātsarvaṃ jagattvameveti
   vastveva siddhimetviti
   yācñā tatrāpi yācñaiva

3 tribhuvanādhipatitvamapīha ya-
   ttṛṇamiva pratibhāti bhavajjuṣaḥ
   kimiva tasya phalaṃ subhakarmaṇo
   bhavati nātha bhavatsmaraṇādṛte

4 yena naiva bhavato'sti vibhinnaṃ
   kiñcanāpi jagatāṃ prabhavaśca
   tvadvijṛmbhitamato'dbhutakarma-
   svapyudeti na tava stutibandhaḥ

5 tvanmayo'smi bhavadarcananiṣṭhaḥ
   sarvadāhamiti cāpyavirāmam
   bhāvayannapi vibho svarasena
   svapnago'pi na tathā kimiva syām

6 ye manāgapi bhavaccaraṇābjo-
   dbhūtasaurabhalavena vimṛṣṭaḥ

138

teṣu visramiva bhavati samastaṃ
bhogajātamamarairapi mṛgyam

hṛdi te na tu vidyate'nyadanya-   7
dvacane karmaṇi cānyadeva śaṃbho
paramārthasato'pyanugraho vā
yadi vā nigraha eka eva kāryaḥ

mūḍho'smi duḥkhakalito'smi jarādidoṣa-   8
bhīto'smi śaktirahito'smi tavāśrito'smi
śambho tathā kalaya śīghramupaimi yena
sarvottamāṃ dhuramapojjhitaduḥkhamārgaḥ

tvatkarṇadeśamadhiśayya mahārghabhāva-   9
mākranditāni mama tucchatarāṇi yānti
vaṃśāntarālapatitāni jalaikadeśa-
khaṇḍāni mauktikamaṇitvamivodvahanti

kimiva ca labhyate bata na tairapi nātha janaiḥ   10
kṣaṇamapi kaitavādapi ca ye tava nāmni ratāḥ
śiśiramayūkhaśekhara tathā kuru yena mama
kṣatamaraṇo'ṇimādikamupaimi yathā vibhavam

śambho sarva śaśaṅkaśekhara śiva tryakṣākṣamālādhara   11
śrīmannugrakapālalāñchana lasadbhīmatriśūlāyudha
kāruṇyāmbunidhe trilokaracanāśīlograśaktyātmaka
śrīkaṇṭhāśu vināśayāśubhabharānādhatsvasiddhiṃ parām

tatkiṃ nātha bhavenna yatra bhagavānnirmātṛtāmaśnute   12
bhāvaḥ syātkimu tasya cetanavato nāśāsti yaṃ śaṅkaraḥ
itthaṃ te parameśvarākṣatamahāśakteḥ sadā saṃśritaḥ
saṃsāre'tra nirantarādhividhuraḥ kliśyāmyahaṃ kevalam

yadyapyatra varapradoddhatatamāḥ pīḍājarāmṛtyavaḥ   13
ete vā kṣaṇamāsatāṃ bahumataḥ śabdādirevāsthiraḥ
tatrāpi spṛhayāmi santatasukhākāṅkṣī ciraṃ sthāsnave
bhogāsvādayutatvadaṅghrikamaladhyānāgrya jīvātave

he nātha praṇatārtināśanapaṭo śreyonidhe dhūrjaṭe   14
duḥkhaikāyatanasya janmamaraṇatrastasya me sāmpratam

taccestasva yathā manojñaviṣayāsvādapradā uttamāḥ
jīvanneva samaśnuve'hamacalāḥ siddhīstvadarcāparaḥ

15　namo mohamahādhvānta-
dhvaṃsanānanyakarmaṇe
sarvaprakāśātiśaya-
prakāśāyendulakṣmaṇe

The Twelfth Song

•

Rahasyanirdeśanāma dvādaśaṃ stotram

sahakāri na kiñcidiṣyate 1
    bhavato na pratibandhakaṃ dṛṣi
bhavataiva hi sarvamāplutaṃ
    kathamadyāpi tathāpi nekṣase

api bhāvagaṇādapīndriya- 2
    pracayādapyavabodhamadhyataḥ
prabhavantamapi svataḥ sadā
    p'aripaśyeyamapoḍhaviśvakam

kathaṃ te jāyerankathamapi ca te darśanapathaṃ 3
    vrajeyuḥ kenāpi prakṛtimahatāṅkena khacitaḥ
tathotthāyotthāya sthalajalatṛṇāderakhilataḥ
    padārthadyānsṛṣṭisravadamṛtapūrairvikirasi

sākṣatkṛtabhavadrūpapaprasṛtāmṛtatarpitāḥ 4
    unmūlitatṛṣo mattā vicaranti yathāruci

na tadā na sadā na caikade- 5
    tyapi sā yatra na kāladhīrbhavet
tadidaṃ bhavadīyadarśanaṃ
    na ca nityaṃ na ca kathyate'nyathā

tvadvilokanasamutkacetaso 6
    yogasiddhiriyatī sadāstu me
yadviśeyamabhisandhimātrata-
    stvatsudhāsadanamarcanāya te

Twelfth Song

7   nirvikalpabhavadīyadarśana-
    praptiphullamanasāṃ mahātmanām
    ullasanti vimalāni helayā
    ceṣṭitāni ca vacāṃsi ca sphuṭam

8   bhavanbhavadīyapādayo-
    rnivasannantara eva nirbhayaḥ
    bhavabhūmiṣu tāsu tāsvahaṃ
    prabhumarceyamanargalakriyaḥ

9   bhavadaṅghrisaroruhodare
    parilīno galitaparaiṣaṇaḥ
    atimātramadhūpayogataḥ
    paritṛpto vicareyamicchayā

10 yasya dambhādiva bhavatpūjāsaṅkalpa utthitaḥ
    tasyāpyavaśyamuditaṃ sannidhānaṃ tavocitam

11 bhagavannitarānapekṣiṇā
    nitarāmekarasena cetasā
    sulabhaṃ sakalopaśāyinaṃ
    prabhumātṛpti pibeyamasmi kim

12 tvayā nirākṛtam sarvaṃ heyametattadeva tu
    tvanmayaṃ samupādeyamityayaṃ sārasaṃgrahaḥ

13 bhavato'ntaracāri bhāvajātaṃ
    prabhuvanmukhyatayaiva pūjitaṃ tat
    bhavato bahirapyabhāvamātrā
    kathamīśān bhavetsamarcyate vā

14 niḥśabdaṃ nirvikalpaṃ ca nirvyākṣepamathānisam
    kṣobhe'pyadhyakṣamī kṣeyaṃ tryakṣa tvāmeva sarvataḥ

15 prakaṭaya nijadhāma deva yasmiṃ-
    stvamasi sadā parameśvarīsametaḥ
    prabhucaraṇarajaḥsamānakakṣyāḥ
    kimaviśvāsapadaṃ bhanti bhṛtyāḥ

16 darśanapathamupayāto'pyapasarasi
    kuto mameśa bhṛtyasya

kṣaṇamātrakamiha na bhavasi
kasya na jantordṛśorviṣayaḥ

aikyasaṃvidamṛtācchadhārayā   17
santataprasṛtayā kadā vibho
plāvanāt paramabhedamānayaṃ-
stvāṃ nijaṃ ca vapurāpnuyāṃ mudam

ahamityamuto'varuddhalokā-   18
dbhavadīyātpratipattisārato me
aṇumātrakameva viśvaniṣṭhaṃ
ghaṭatāṃ yena bhaveyamarcitā te

aparimitarūpamahaṃ   19
taṃ taṃ bhāvaṃ pratikṣaṇaṃ paśyan
tvāmeva viśvarūpaṃ
nijanāthaṃ sādhu paśyeyam

bhavadaṅgagataṃ tameva kasmā-   20
nna manaḥ paryaṭatīṣṭamarthamartham
prakṛtikṣatirasti no tathāsya
mama cecchā paripūryate paraiva

śataśaḥ kila te tavānubhāvā-   21
dbhagavanke'pyamunaiva cakṣuṣā ye
api hālikaceṣṭayā carantaḥ
paripaśyanti bhavadvapuḥ sadāgre

na sā matirudeti yā na bhavati tvadicchāmayī   22
sadā śubhamathetaradbhagavataivamācaryate
ato'smi bhavadātmako bhuvi yathā tathā sañcaran
sthito'niśamabādhitatvadamalaṅghripūjotsavaḥ

bhavadīyagabhīrabhāṣiteṣu   23
pratibhā samyagudetu me puro'taḥ
tadanuṣṭhitaśaktirapyatasta-
dbhavadarcāvyasanaṃ ca nirvirāmam

vyavahārapade'pi sarvadā   24
pratibhātvarthakalāpa eṣa mām

143

bhavato'vayavo yathā na tu
svata evādaraṇīyatāṃ gataḥ

25 manasi svarasena yatra tatra
pracaratyapyahamasya gocareṣu
prasṛto'pyavilola eva yuṣma-
tparicaryācaturaḥ sadā bhaveyam

26 bhagavanbhavadicchayaiva dāsa-
stava jāto'smi parasya nātra śaktiḥ
kathameṣa tathāpi vaktrabimbaṃ
tava paśyāmi na jātu citrametat

27 samutsukāstvāṃ prati ye bhavantaṃ
pratyartharūpādavalokayanti
teṣāmaho kiṃ tadupasthitaṃ syāt
kiṃ sādhanaṃ vā phalitaṃ bhavettat

28 bhāvā bhāvatayā santu
bhavadbhāvena me bhava
tathā na kiñcidapyastu
na kiñcidbhavato'nyathā

29 yanna kiñcidapi tanna kiñcidapyastu kiñcidapi kiñcideva me
sarvathā bhavatu tāvatā bhavān
sarvato bhavati labdhapūjitaḥ

The Thirteenth Song

•

Saṃgrahastotranāma
trayodaśaṃ stotram

saṃgrahena sukhaduḥkhalakṣaṇaṃ   1
    māṃ prati sthitamidaṃ śṛṇu prabho
saukhyameṣa bhavatā samāgamaḥ
    svāminā viraha eva duḥkhitā

antarapyatitarāmaṇīyasī   2
    yā tvadaprathanakālikāsti me
tāmapīśa parimṛjya sarvataḥ
    svaṃ svarūpamamalaṃ prakāśaya

tāvake vapuṣi viśvanirbhare   3
    citsudhārasamaye niratyaye
tiṣṭhataḥ satatamarcataḥ prabhuṃ
    jīvitaṃ mṛtamathānyadastu me

īśvaro'hamahameva rūpavān   4
    paṇḍito'smi subhago'smi ko'paraḥ
matsamo'sti jagatīti śobhate
    mānitā tvadanurāgiṇaḥ param

devadeva bhavadadvayāmṛtā-   5
    khyātisaṃharaṇalabdhajanmanā
tadyathāsthitapadārthasaṃvidā
    māṃ kuruṣva caraṇārcanocitam

dhyāyate tadanu dṛśyate tataḥ   6
    spṛśyate ca parameśvaraḥ svayam

yatra pūjanamahotsavaḥ sa me
sarvadāstu bhavato'nubhāvataḥ

7   yadyathāsthitapadārthadarśanaṃ
yuṣmadarcanamahotsavaśca yaḥ
yugmametaditaretarāśrayaṃ
bhaktiśāliṣu sadā vijṛmbhate

8   tattadindriyamukhena santataṃ
yuṣmadarcanarasāyanāsavam
sarvabhāvacaṣakeṣu pūrite-
ṣvāpibannapi bhaveyamunmadaḥ

9   anyavedyamaṇumātramasti na
svaprakāśamakhilaṃ vijṛmbhate
yatra nātha bhavataḥ pure sthitaṃ
tatra me kuru sadā tavārcituḥ

10   dāsadhāmni viniyojito'pyahaṃ
svecchayaiva parameśvara tvayā
darśanena na kimasmi pātritaḥ
pādasaṃvahanakarmaṇāpi vā

11   śaktipātasamaye vicāraṇaṃ
prāptamīśa na karoṣi karhicit
adya māṃ prati kimāgataṃ yataḥ
svaprakāśanavidhau vilambase

12   tatra tatra viṣaye bahirvibhā-
tyantare ca parameśvarīyutam
tvāṃ jagattritayanirbharaṃ sadā
lokayeya nijapāṇipūjitam

13   svāmisaudhamabhisandhimātrato
nirvibandhamadhiruhya sarvadā
syāṃ prasādaparamāmṛtāsavā-
pānakeliparilabdhanirvṛtiḥ

14   yatsamastasubhagārthavastuṣu
sparśamātravidhinā camatkṛtim

tāṃ samarpayati tena te vapuḥ
pūjayantyacalabhaktiśālinaḥ

sphārayasyakhilamātmanā sphuran   15
viśvamāmṛśasi rūpamāmṛśan
yatsvayaṃ nijarasena ghurṇase
tatsamullasati bhāvamaṇḍalam

yo'vikalpamidamarthamaṇḍalaṃ   16
paśyatīśa nikhilaṃ bhavadvapuḥ
svātmapakṣaparipūrite jaga-
tyasya nityasukhinaḥ kuto bhayam

kaṇṭhakoṇaviniviṣṭamīśa te   17
kālakūṭamapi me mahāmṛtam
apyupāttamamṛtaṃ bhavadvapu-
rbhedavṛtti yadi rocate na me

tvatpralāpamayaraktagītikā-   18
nityayuktavadanopaśobhitaḥ
syāmathāpi bhavadarcanakriyā-
preyasīparigatāśayaḥ sadā

īhitaṃ na bata pārameśvaraṃ   19
śakyate gaṇayituṃ tathā ca me
dattamapyamṛtanirbharaṃ vapuḥ
svaṃ na pātumanumanyate tathā

tvāmagādhamavikalpamadvayaṃ   20
svaṃ svarūpamakhilārthaghasmaram
āviśannahamumeśa sarvadā
pūjayeyamabhisaṃstuvīya ca

The Fourteenth Song

•

Jayastotranāma caturdaśaṃ stotram

1 jayalakṣmīnidhānasya nijasya svāminaḥ puraḥ
jayoddhoṣaṇapīyūṣarasamāsvādaye kṣaṇam

2 jayaikarudraikaśiva mahādeva maheśvara
pārvatīpraṇayiñśarva sarvagīrvāṇapūrvaja

3 jaya trailokyanāthaikalāñchanālikalocana
jaya pītartalokārtikālakūṭāṅkakandhara

4 jaya mūrtatriśaktyātmiśataśūlollasatkara
jayecchāmātrasiddārthapūjārhacaraṇāmbuja

5 jaya śobhaśatasyandilokottaravapurdhara
jayaikajaṭikākṣīṇagaṅgākṛtyāttabhasmaka

6 jaya kṣīrodaparyastajyotsnācchāyānulepana
jayeśvarāṅgasaṅgottharatnakāntāhimaṇḍana

7 jayākṣayaikaśītāṃśukalāsadṛśasaṃśraya
jaya gaṅgāsadārbdhaviśvaiśvaryābhiṣecana

8 jayādharāṅgasaṃsparśapāvanīkṛtagokula
jaya bhaktimadābaddhagoṣṭhīniyatasannidhe

9 jaya svecchātapodeśavipralambhitabāliśa
jaya gaurīpariṣvaṅgayogyasaubhāgyabhājana

10 jaya bhaktirasārdrārdrabhāvopāyanalampaṭa
jaya bhaktimadoddāmabhaktavāṅnṛttatoṣita

jaya brahmādideveśaprabhāvaprabhavavyaya 11
jayalokeśvaraśreṇīśirovidhṛtaśāsana

jaya sarvajagannyastasvamudrāvyaktavaibhava 12
jayātmadānaparyantaviśveśvara maheśvara

jaya trailokyasargecchāvasarāsaddvitīyaka 13
jayaiśvaryabharodvāhadevīmātrasahāyaka

jayākramasamākrāntasamastabhuvanatraya 14
jayāvigītamābālagīyamāneśvaradhvane

jayānukampādiguṇānapekṣasahajonnate 15
jaya bhīṣmamahāmṛtyughaṭanāpūrvabhairava

jaya viśvakṣayoccaṇḍakriyāniṣparipanthika 16
jaya śreyaḥśataguṇānuganāmānukīrtana

jaya helāvitīrnaitadamṛtākarasāgara 17
jaya viśvakṣayakṣepikṣaṇakopāśuśukṣaṇe

jaya mohāndhakārāndhajīvalokaikadīpaka 18
jaya prasuptajagatījāgarūkādhipūruṣa

jaya dehādrikuñjāntarnikūjañjīvajīvaka 19
jaya sanmānasavyomavilāsivarasārasa

jaya jāmbūnadodagradhātūdbhavagirīśvara 20
jaya pāpiṣu nindolkāpātanotpātacandramaḥ

jaya kaṣṭatapaḥkliṣṭamunidevadurāsada 21
jaya sarvadaśārūḍhabhaktimallokalokita

jaya svasampatprasarapatrīkṛtanijāśrita 22
jaya prapannajanatālālanaikaprayojana

jaya sargasthitidhvaṃsakāraṇaikāvadānaka 23
jaya bhaktimadālolalīlotpalamagotsava

149

Fourteenth Song

24   jaya jayabhājana jaya jitajanma-
       jarāmaraṇa jaya jagajjyeṣṭha
     jaya jaya jaya jaya jaya jaya jaya
      jaya jaya jaya jaya jaya jaya tryakṣa

The Fifteenth Song

•

Bhaktistotranāma pañcadaśaṃ stotram

trimalakṣālino granthāḥ santi tatpāragāstathā 1
yoginaḥ paṇḍitāḥ svasthāstvadbhaktā eva tatvataḥ

māyīyakālaniyatirāgādyāhāratarpitāḥ 2
caranti sukhino nātha bhaktimanto jagattaṭe

rudanto vā hasanto vā tvāmuccaiḥ pralapantyamī 3
bhaktāḥ stutipadoccāropacārāḥ pṛthageva te

na virakto na cāpīśo mokṣākāṅkṣī tvadarcakaḥ 4
bhaveyamapi tūdriktabhaktyāsavarasonmadaḥ

bāhyaṃ hṛdaya evāntarabhihṛtyaiva yo'rcati 5
tvāmīśa bhaktipīyūṣarasapūrairnamāmi tam

dharmādharmātmanorantaḥ kriyayorjñānayostathā 6
sukhaduḥkhātmanorbhaktāḥ kimapyāsvādayantyaho

carācarapitaḥ svāmin apyandhā api kuṣṭhinaḥ 7
śobhante paramuddāmabhavadbhaktivibhūṣaṇāḥ

śiloñchapicchakaśipuvicchāyāṅgā api prabho 8
bhavadbhaktimahoṣmaṇo rājarājamapīśate

sudhārdrāyāṃ bhavadbhaktau luṭhatāpyārurukṣuṇā 9
cetasaiva vibho'rcanti kecittvāmabhitaḥ sthitāḥ

rakṣaṇīyaṃ vardhanīyaṃ bahumānyamidaṃ prabho 10
saṃsāradurgatiharaṃ bhavadbhaktimahādhanam

151

Fifteenth Song

11 nātha te bhaktajanatā yadyapi tvayi rāgiṇī
    tathāpīrṣyāṃ vihāyāsyāstuṣṭāstu svāminī sadā

12 bhavadbhāvaḥ puro bhāvī prāpte tvadbhaktisambhave
    labdhe dugdhamahākumbhe hatā dadhani gṛdhnutā

13 kimiyaṃ na siddhiratulā
    kiṃ vā mukhyaṃ na saukhyamāsravati
    bhaktirupacīyamānā
    yeyaṃ śambhoḥ sadātanī bhavati

14 manasi maline madīye
    magnā tvadbhaktimaṇilatā kaṣṭam
    na nijānapi tanute tān
    apauruṣeyānsvasampadullāsān

15 bhaktirbhagavati bhavati
    trilokanāthe nanūttamā siddhiḥ
    kintvaṇimādikavirahāt
    saiva na pūrṇeti cintā me

16 bāhyato'ntarapi cotkaṭonmiṣa-
    ttryambakastavakasaurabhāḥ śubhāḥ
    vāsayantyapi viruddhavāsanān
    yogino nikaṭavāsino'khilān

17 jyotirasti kathayāpi na kiṃci-
    dviśvamapyatisuṣuptamaśeṣam
    yatra nātha śivarātripade'smin
    nityamarcayati bhaktajanastvām

18 sattvaṃ satyaguṇe śive bhagavati sphārībhavatvarcane
    cūḍāyāṃ vilasantu śaṅkarapadaprodyadrajaḥsañcayāḥ
    rāgādismṛtivāsanāmapi samucchettuṃ tamo jṛmbhatāṃ
    śambho me bhavatāttvadātmavilaye traiguṇyavargo'thavā

19 saṃsārādhvā sudūraḥ kharataravividhavyādhidagdhāṅgayaṣṭiḥ
    bhogā naivopabhuktā yadapi sukhamabhūjjātu nanno cirāya
    itthaṃ vyartho'smi jātaḥ śaśidharacaraṇākrāntikāntottamāṅga-
    stvadbhaktaśceti tanme kuru sapadi mahāsampado dīrghadīrghāḥ

The Sixteenth Song

•

Pāśānudbhedanāma ṣoḍaśaṃ stotram

na kiñcideva lokānāṃ bhavadāvaraṇaṃ prati   1
na kiñcideva bhaktānāṃ bhavadāvaraṇaṃ prati

apyupāyakramaprāpyaḥ saṅkulo'pi viśeṣaṇaiḥ   2
bhaktibhājāṃ bhavānātmā sakṛcchuddho'vabhāsate

jayanto'pi hasantyete jitā api hasanti ca   3
bhavadbhaktisudhāpānamattāḥ ke'pyeva ye prabho

śuṣkakaṃ maiva siddheya maiva mucyeya vāpi tu   4
svādiṣṭhaparakāṣṭāptatvadbhaktirasanirbharaḥ

yathaivajñātapūrvo'yaṃ bhavadbhaktiraso mama   5
ghaṭitastadvadīśāna sa eva paripuṣyatu

satyena bhagavannānyaḥ prārthanāprasaro'sti me   6
kevalaṃ sa tathā ko'pi bhaktyāveśo'stu me sadā

bhaktikṣīvo'pi kupyeyaṃ bhavāyānuśayīya ca   7
tathā haseyaṃ udyāṃ ca raṭeyaṃ ca śivetyalam

viṣamastho'pi svastho'pi rudannapi hasannapi   8
gambhīro'pi vicitto'pi bhaveyaṃ bhaktitaḥ prabho

bhaktānāṃ nāsti saṃvedyaṃ tvadantaryadi vā bahiḥ   9
ciddharmā yatra na bhavānnirvikalpaḥ sthitaḥ svayam

bhaktā nindānukare'pi tavāmṛtakaṇairiva   10
hṛṣyantyevāntarāviddhāstīkṣṇaromāñcasūcibhiḥ

Sixteenth Song

11   duḥkhāpi vedanā bhaktimatāṃ bhogāya kalpate
yeṣāṃ sudhārdrā sarvaiva saṃvittvaccandrikāmayī

12   yatra tatroparuddhānāṃ bhaktānāṃ bahirantare
nirvyājaṃ tvadvapuḥsparśarasāsvādasukhaṃ samam

13   taveśa bhakterarcāyāṃ dainyāṃśaṃ dvayasaṃśrayam
vilupyāsvādayantyeke vapuracchaṃ sudhāmayam

14   bhrāntāstīrthadṛśo bhinnā bhrāntereva hi bhinnatā
niṣpratidvandvi vastvekaṃ bhaktānāṃ tvaṃ tu rājase

15   mānāvamānarāgādiniṣpākavimalaṃ manaḥ
yasyāsau bhaktimāṃllokatulyaśīlaḥ kathaṃ bhavet

16   rāgadveṣandhakāro'pi yeṣāṃ bhaktitviṣā jitaḥ
teṣāṃ mahīyasāmagre katame jñānaśālinaḥ

17   yasya bhaktisudhāsnānapānādividhisādhanam
tasya prārabdhamadhyāntadaśāsūccaiḥ sukhāsikā

18   kīrtyaścintāpadaṃ mṛgyaḥ pūjyo yena tvameva tat
bhavadbhaktimatāṃ ślāghyā lokayātrā bhavanmayī

19   muktisaṃjñā vipakvāyā bhaktereva tvayi prabho
tasyāmādyadaśārūḍhā muktakalpā vayaṃ tataḥ

20   duḥkhāgamo'pi bhūyānme tvadbhaktibharitātmanaḥ
tvatparācī vibho mā bhūdapi saukhyaparamparā

21   tvaṃ bhaktyā prīyase bhaktiḥ prīte tvayi ca nātha yat
tadanyonyāśrayaṃ yuktaṃ yathā vettha tvameva tat

22   sākāro vā nirākaro vantarvā bahireva vā
bhaktimattātmanāṃ nātha sarvathāsi sudhāmayaḥ

23   asminneva jagatyantarbhavadbhaktimataḥ prati
harṣaprakāśanaphalamanyadeva jagatsthitam

24   guhye bhaktiḥ pare bhaktirbhaktirviśvamaheśvare
tvayi śambhau śive deva bhaktirnāma kimapyaho

bhaktirbhaktiḥ pare bhaktirbhaktirnāma samutkaṭā   25
tāraṃ viraumi yattīvrā bhaktirme'stu paraṃ tvayi

yato'smi sarvaśobhānāṃ prasavāvanirīśa tat   26
tvayi lagnamanarghaṃ syādratnam vā yadi vā tṛṇam

āvedakādā ca vedyādyeṣāṃ saṃvedanādhvani   27
bhavatā na viyogo'sti te jayanti bhavajjuṣaḥ

saṃsārasadaso bāhye kaiścittvaṃ parirabhyase   28
svāminparaistu tatraiva tāmyadbhistyaktayantraṇaiḥ

pānāśanaprasādhana-   29
  sambhuktasamastaviśvayā śivayā
  pralayotsavasarabhasayā
  dṛḍhamupagūḍhaṃ śivaṃ vande

parameśvaratā jayatyapūrvā   30
  tava viśveśa yadīśitavyaśūnyā
  aparāpi tathaiva te yayedaṃ
  jagadābhāti yathā tathā na bhāti

The Seventeenth Song

•

Divyakrīḍābahumānanāma saptadaśaṃ stotram

1   aho ko'pi jayatyeṣa svāduḥ pūjāmahotsavaḥ
yato'mṛtarasāsvādamasrūṇyapi dadatyalam

2   vyāpārāḥ siddhidāḥ sarve ye tvatpūjāpuraḥsarāḥ
bhaktānāṃ tvanmayāḥ sarve svayaṃ siddhaya eva te

3   sarvadā sarvabhāveṣu yugapatsarvarūpiṇam
tvāmarcayantyaviśrantaṃ ye mamaite'dhidevatāḥ

4   dhyānāyasatiraskārasiddhastvatsparśanotsavaḥ
pūjāvidhiriti khyāto bhaktānāṃ sa sadāstu me

5   bhaktānāṃ samatāsāraviṣuvatsamayaḥ sadā
tvadbhāvarasapīyūṣarasennaiṣāṃ sadārcanam

6   yasyānārambhaparyantau na ca kālakramaḥ prabho
pūjātmāsau kriyā tasyāḥ kartārastvajjuṣaḥ param

7   brahmādīnāmapīśāste te ca saubhāgyabhāginaḥ
yeṣāṃ svapne'pi mohe'pi sthitastvatpūjanotsavaḥ

8   japatāṃ juhvatāṃ snātāṃ dhyāyatāṃ na ca kevalam
bhaktānāṃ bhavadabhyarcāmaho yāvadyadā tadā

9   bhavatpūjāsudhāsvādasambhogasukhinaḥ sadā
indrādīnāmatha brahmamukhyānāmasti kaḥ samaḥ

jagatkṣobhaikajanake bhavatpūjāmahotsave 10
yatprāpyaṃ prāpyate kiṃcidbhaktā eva vidanti tat

tvaddhāmni cinmaye sthitvā ṣaṭtriṃśattattvakarmabhiḥ 11
kāyavākcittaceṣṭādyairarcaye tvāṃ sadā vibho

bhavatpūjāmayāsaṅgasambhogasukhino mama 12
prayātu kālaḥ sakalo'pyananto'pīyadarthaye

bhavatpūjāmṛtarasābhogalampaṭata vibho 13
vivardhatāmanudinaṃ sadā ca phalatāṃ mama

jagadvilayasañjātasudhaikarasanirbhare 14
tvadabdhau tvāṃ mahātmānamarcannāsīya sarvadā

aśeṣavāsanāgranthivicchedasaralaṃ sadā 15
mano nivedyate bhaktaiḥ svādu pūjāvidhau tava

adhiṣṭhāyaiva viṣayānimāḥ karaṇavṛttayaḥ 16
bhaktānāṃ preṣayanti svatpūjārthamamṛtāsavam

bhaktānāṃ bhaktisaṃvegamahoṣmavivaśātmanām 17
ko'nyo nirvāṇahetuḥ syāttvatpūjāmṛtamajjanāt

satataṃ tvatpadābhyarcāsudhāpānamahotsavaḥ 18
tvatprasādaikasamprāptiheturme nātha kalpatām

anubhūyāsamīśāna pratikarma kṣaṇātkṣaṇam 19
bhavatpūjāmṛtāpānamadāsvādamahāmudam

dṛṣṭartha eva bhaktānāṃ bhavatpūjāmahodyamaḥ 20
tadaiva yadasambhāvyaṃ sukhamāsvādayanti te

yāvanna labdhastvatpūjāsudhāsvādamahotsavaḥ 21
tāvannāsvādito manye lavo'pi sukhasampadaḥ

bhaktānāṃ viṣayanveṣābhāsāyāsādvinaiva sā 22
ayatnasiddhaṃ tvaddhāmasthitiḥ pūjāsu jāyate

na prāpyamasti bhaktānāṃ nāpyeṣāmasti durlabham 23
kevalaṃ vicarantyete bhavatpūjāmadonmadāḥ

24 aho bhaktibharodāracetasāṃ varada tvayi
    slāghyaḥ pūjāvidhiḥ ko'pi yo na yācñākalaṃkitaḥ

25 kā nā śobhā na ko hlādaḥ kā samṛddhirna vāparā
    ko vā na mokṣaḥ ko'pyeṣa mahādevo yadarcyate

26 antarullasadacchācchabhaktipīyūṣapoṣitam
    bhavatpūjopayogāya śarīramidamastu me

27 tvatpādapūjāsambhogaparatantraḥ sadā vibho
    bhūyāsaṃ jagatāmīśa ekaḥ svacchandaceṣṭitaḥ

28 tvaddhyānadarśanasparśatṛṣi keṣāmapi prabho
    jāyate śītalasvādu bhavatpūjāmahāsaraḥ

29 yathā tvameva jagataḥ pūjāsambhogabhājanam
    tatheśa bhaktimāneva pūjāsambhogabhājanam

30 ko'pyasau jayati svāminbhavatpūjāmahotsavaḥ
    ṣaṭtriṃśato'pi tattvānāṃ kṣobho yatrollasatyalam

31 namastebhyo vibho yeṣāṃ bhaktipīyūṣavāriṇā
    pūjyānyeva bhavanti tvatpūjopakaraṇānyapi

32 pūjārambhe vibho dhyātvā mantrādheyāṃ tvadātmatām
    svātmanyeva pare bhaktā mānti harṣeṇa na kvacit

33 rājyalābhādivotphullaiḥ kaiścitpūjāmahotsave
    sudhāsavena sakalā jagatī saṃvibhajyate

34 pūjāmṛtāpānamayo yeṣāṃ bhogaḥ pratikṣaṇam
    kiṃ devā uta muktāste kiṃ vā ke'pyeva te janāḥ

35 pūjopakaraṇībhūtaviśvaveśena gauravam
    aho kimapi bhaktānāṃ kimapyeva ca lāghavam

36 pūjāmayākṣavikṣepakṣobhādevāmṛtodgamaḥ
    bhaktānāṃ kṣīrajaladhikṣobhādiva divaukasām

37 pūjāṃ kecana manyante dhenuṃ kāmadughāmiva
    sudhādhārādhikarasāṃ dhayantyantarmukhāḥ pare

bhaktānāmakṣavikṣepo'pyeṣa saṃsārasaṃmataḥ 38
upanīya kimapyantaḥ puṣṇātyarcāmahotsavam

bhaktikṣobhavaśādīśa svātmabhūte'rcanaṃ tvayi 39
citraṃ dainyāya no yāvaddīnatāyāḥ paraṃ phalam

upacārapadaṃ pūjā keṣāṃcittvatpadāptaye 40
bhaktānāṃ bhavadaikātmyanirvṛttiprasarastu saḥ

apyasambaddharūpārcā bhaktyunmādanirargalaiḥ 41
vitanyamānā labhate pratiṣṭhāṃ tvayi kāmapi

svādubhaktirasāsvādastabdhībhūtamanaścyutām 42
śambho tvameva lalitaḥ pūjānāṃ kila bhājanam

paripūrṇāni śuddhāni bhaktimanti sthirāṇi ca 43
bhavatpūjāvidhau nātha sādhanāni bhavantu me

aśeṣapūjāsatkośe tvatpūjākarmaṇi prabho 44
aho karaṇavṛndasya kāpi lakṣmīrvijṛmbhate

eṣā peśalimā nātha tavaiva kila dṛśyate 45
viśveśvaro'pi bhṛtyairyadarcyase yaśca labhyase

sadāmurttāda mūrttādva bhāvādyadvāpyabhāvataḥ 46
uttheyānme praśastasya bhavatpūjāmahotsavaḥ

kāmakrodhābhimānaistvāmupaharīkṛtaiḥ sadā 47
ye'rcayanti namastebhyasteṣāṃ tuṣṭo'smi tattvataḥ

jayatyeṣa bhavadbhaktibhājāṃ pūjāvidhiḥ paraḥ 48
yastṛṇaiḥ kriyamāno'pi ratnairevopakalpate

The Eighteenth Song

•

Āviṣkāranāma aṣṭādaśaṃ stotram

1   jagato'ntarato bhavantamāptvā
         punaretadbhavato'ntarāllabhante
         jagadīśa tavaiva bhaktibhājo
         na hi teṣāmiha dūrato'sti kiñcit

2   kvacideva bhavān kvacidbhavānī
         sakalārthakramagarbhiṇī pradhānā
         paramārthapade tu naiva devyā
         bhavato nāpi jatattrayasya bhedaḥ

3   no jānate subhagamapyavalepavanto
         lokāḥ prayatnasubhagā nikhila hi bhāvāḥ
         cetaḥ punaryadidamudyatamapyavaiti
         naivātmarūpamiha hā tadaho hato'smi

4   bhavanmayasvātmanivāsalabdha-
         sampadbharābhyarcitayuṣmadaṅghriḥ
         na bhojanācchādanamapyajasra-
         mapekṣate yastamahaṃ nato'smi

5   sadā bhavaddehanivāsasvastho-
         'pyantaḥ paraṃ dahyata eṣa lokaḥ
         tavecchayā tatkuru me yathātra
         tvadarcanānandamayo bhaveyam

6   svarasoditayuṣmadaṅghripadma-
         dvayapūjāmṛtapānasaktacittaḥ
         sakārthacayeṣvahaṃ bhaveyam
         sukhasaṃsparśanamātralokayātraḥ

sakalavyavahāragocare 7
sphuṭamantaḥ spurati tvayi prabho
upayāntyapayānti cāniśam
mama vastūni vibhāntu sarvadā

satatameva tavaiva pure'thavā- 8
pyarahito vicareyamahaṃ tvayā
kṣaṇalavo'pyathamā sma bhavet sa me
na vijaye nanu yatra bhavanmayaḥ

bhavadaṅgaparisravatsuśītā- 9
mṛtapūrairbharite samantato'pi
bhavadarcanasampadeha bhaktā-
stava saṃsārasaro'ntare caranti

mahāmantratarucchāyāśītale tvanmahāvane 10
nijātmani sadā nātha vaseyaṃ tava pūjakaḥ

prativastu samastajīvataḥ 11
pratibhāsi pratibhāmayo yathā
mama nātha tathā puraḥ prathāṃ
vraja netratrayaśūlaśobhitaḥ

abhimānacarūpahārato 12
mamatābhaktibhareṇa kalpitāt
paritoṣagataḥ kadā bhavān
mama sarvatra bhaved dṛśaḥ padam

nivasanparamāmṛtābdhimadhye 13
bhavadarcāvidhimātramagnacittaḥ
sakalaṃ janavṛttamācareyaṃ
rasayansarvata eva kiñcanāpi

bhavadīyamihāstu vastu tattvaṃ 14
vivarītuṃ ka ivātra pātramarthe
idameva hi nāmarūpaceṣṭā-
dyasamaṃ te harate haro'si yasmāt

śāntaye na sukhalipsutā manā- 15
gbhaktisambhṛtamadeṣu taiḥ prabhoḥ

      mokṣamārgaṇaphalāpi nārthanā
      smaryate hṛdayahāriṇaḥ puraḥ

16   jāgaretaradaśāthavā parā
      yāpi kācana manāgavasthiteḥ
      bhaktibhājanajanasya sākhilā
      tvatsanāthamanaso mahotsavaḥ

17   āmano'kṣavalayasya vṛttayaḥ
      sarvataḥ śithilavṛttayo'pi tāḥ
      tvāmavāpya dṛḍhadīrghasaṃvido
      nātha bhaktidhanasoṣmaṇāṃ katham

18   na ca vibhinnamasṛjyata kiñcida-
      styatha sukhetaradatra na nirmitam
      atha ca duḥkhi ca bhedi ca sarvathā-
      pyasamavismayadhāma namo'stu te

19   kharaniṣedhakhadāmṛtapūraṇo-
      cchalitadhautavikalpamalasya me
      dalitadurjayasaṃśayavairiṇa-
      stvadavalokanamastu nirantaram

20   sphuṭamaviśa māmathāviśeyaṃ
      satataṃ nātha bhavantamasmi yasmāt
      rabhasena vapustavaiva sākṣā-
      tparamāsattigataḥ samarcayeyam

21   tvayi na stutiśaktirasti kasyā-
      pyathavāstyeva yato'tisundaro'si
      satataṃ punararthitaṃ mamaita-
      dyadaviśrānti vilokayeyamīśam

The Nineteenth Song

•

Udyotanābhidhānam ekonaviṃśaṃ stotram

prārthanābhūmikātītavicitraphaladāyakaḥ   1
jayatyapūrvavṛttāntaḥ śivaḥ satkalpapādapaḥ

sarvavastunicayaikanidhānā-   2
tsvātmanastvadakhilaṃ kila labhyam
asya me punarasau nijā ātmā
na tvameva ghaṭase paramāstām

jñānakarmamayacidvapurātmā   3
sarvathaiṣa parameśvara eva
syādvapastu nikhileṣu padārthe-
ṣveṣu nāma na bhavetkimutānyat

viṣamārtimuṣānena phalena tvadṛgātmanā   4
abhilīya pathā nātha mamāstu tvanmayī gatiḥ

bhavadamalacaraṇacintāratnalatā-   5
laṅkṛtā kaḍā siddhiḥ
siddhajanamānasānāṃ vismayajananī
ghaṭeta mama bhavataḥ

karhi nātha vimalaṃ mukhabimbaṃ   6
tāvakaṃ samavalokayitāsmi
yatsravatyamṛtapūramapūrvaṃ
yo nimajjayati viśvamaśeṣam

7   dhyātamātramuditaṃ tava rūpaṃ
      karhi nātha paramāmṛtapūraiḥ
      pūrayettvadavibhedavimokṣā-
      khyātidūravivarāṇi sadā me

8   tvadīyānuttararasāsaṅgasantyaktacāpalam
      nādyāpi me mano nātha karhi syādastu śīghrataḥ

9   mā śuṣkakaṭukānyeva paraṃ sarvāṇi sarvadā
      tavopahṛtya labdhāni dvandvānyapyāpatantu me

10   nātha sāmmukhyamāyāntu viśuddhāstava raśmayaḥ
      yāvatkāyamanastāpatamobhiḥ parilupyatām

11   deva prasīda yāvanme tvanmārgaparipanthikāḥ
      paramārthamuṣo vaśyā bhūyāsurguṇataskarāḥ

12   tvadbhaktisudhāsārai-
         rmānasamāpūryatāṃ mamāśu vibho
      yāvadimā uhyantāṃ
         niḥśeṣāsāravāsanāḥ plutvā

13   mokṣadaśāyāṃ bhakti-
         stvayi kuta iva martyadharmiṇo'pi na sā
      rājati tato'nurūpā-
         māropaya siddhibhūmikāmaja mām

14   siddhilavalābhalubdhaṃ
         māmavalepena mā vibho saṃsthāḥ
      kṣāmastvadbhaktimukhe
         prollasadaṇimādipakṣato mokṣaḥ

15   dāsasya me prasīdatu
         bhagavānetāvadeva nanu yāce
      dātā tribhuvananātho
         yasya na tanmādṛśāṃ dṛśo viṣayaḥ

16   tvadvapuḥsmṛtisudharasapūrṇe
         mānase tava padāmbujayugmam
      māmake vikasadastu sadaiva
         prasravanmadhu kimapyatilokam

asti me prabhurasau janaki'tha   17
    tryambako'tha janani ca bhavānī
na dvitīya iha ko'pi mamastī-
    tyeva nirvṛtatamo vicareyam

The Twentieth Song

•

Carvaṇābhidhānaṃ viṃśaṃ stotram

1   nāthaṃ tribhuvananāthaṃ bhūtisitaṃ trinayanaṃ triśūladharam
     upavītīkṛtabhoginamindukalāśekharaṃ vande

2   naumi nijatanuvinismaradaṃśukapariveṣadhavalaparidhānam
     vilasatkapālamālākalpitanṛttotsavākalpam

3   vande tān daivataṃ yeṣāṃ haraśceṣṭā harocitāḥ
     haraikapravaṇāḥ prāṇāḥ sadā saubhāgyasadmanām

4   krīḍitaṃ tava maheśvaratāyāḥ pṛṣṭhato'nyadidameva yathaitat
     iṣṭamātraghaṭiteṣvavadāneṣvātmanā paramupāyamupaimi

5   tvaddhāmni viśvavandye'sminniyati krīḍane sati
     tava nātha kiyān bhūyānnānandarasasambhavaḥ

6   kathaṃ sa subhago mā bhūdyo gauryā vallabho haraḥ
     haro'pi mā bhūdatha kiṃ gauryāḥ paramavallabhaḥ

7   dhyānāmṛtamayaṃ yasya svātmamūlamanaśvaram
     saṃvillatāstathārūpāstasya kasyāpi sattaroḥ

8   bhaktikaṇḍūsamullāsāvasare parameśvara
     mahānikaṣapāṣāṇasthūṇā pūjaiva jāyate

9   sadā sṛṣṭivinodāya sadā sthitisukhāsine
     sadā tribhuvanāhāratṛptāya svāmine namaḥ

10   na kvāpi gatvā hitvāpi na kiṃcididameva ye
     bhavyaṃ tvaddhāma paśyanti bhavyāstebhyo namo namaḥ

166

bhaktilakṣmīsamṛddhānāṃ kimanyadupayācitam 11
etayā vā daridrāṇāṃ kimanyadupayācitam

duḥkhānyapi sukhāyante viṣamapyamṛtāyate 12
mokṣāyate ca saṃsāro yatra mārgaḥ sa śaṅkaraḥ

mūle madhy'vasāne ca nāsti duḥkhaṃ bhavajjuṣāṃ 13
tathāpi vayamīśāna sīdāmaḥ kathamucyatām

jñānayogādinānyeṣāmapyapekṣitumarhati 14
prakāśaḥ svairiṇāmiva bhavān bhaktimatāṃ prabho

bhaktānāṃ nārtayo nāpyastyādhyānaṃ svātmanastava 15
tathāpyasti śivetyetatkimapyeṣāṃ bahirmukhe

sarvābhāsāvabhāso yo vimarśavalito'khilam 16
ahametaditi staumi tāṃ kriyāśaktimīśa te

vartante jantavo'śeṣā api brahmendraviṣṇavaḥ 17
grasamānāstato vande deva viśvaṃ bhavanmayam

sato vināśasambandhānmatparaṃ nikhilaṃ mṛṣā 18
evamevodyate nātha tvayā saṃhāralīlayā

dhyātamātramupatiṣṭhata eva 19
tvadvapurvarada bhaktidhanānām
apyacintyamakhilādbhutacintā-
kartṛtāṃ prati ca te vijayante

tāvakabhaktirasāsava- 20
sekādiva sukhitamarmamaṇḍalasphuritaiḥ
nṛtyati vīrajano niśi
vetālakulaiḥ kṛtotsāhaḥ

ārabdhā bhavadabhinuti- 21
ramunā yenāṅgakena mama śambho
tenāparyantamimaṃ kālaṃ
dṛḍhamakhilameva bhaviṣīṣṭa

Appendix A

Highlights of Pratyabhijñā
(The Doctrine of Recognition)

The literature of what is generally known as Kashmir Śaivism traditionally is divided into three branches known as the Āgama Śāstra, Spanda Śāstra, and Pratyabhijñā Śāstra. These are considered to be varying but interdependent approaches to one religious and philosophical system. Often the whole system is known as Trika Śāstra, indicating the unity of the three branches. Just as often, however, the term Pratyabhijñā, or Doctrine of Recognition, because it embodies the main philosophical works of Kashmir Śaivism, has come to represent the whole. The major figures of the Pratyabhijñā Śāstra are Somānanda (*ca.* A.D. 875-925), Utpaladeva (*ca.* 900-950), and Abhinavagupta (*ca.* 950-1000); the three have been labeled respectively as "the founder, the systematizer, and the expounder" of Pratyabhijñā.[1]

The term *pratyabhijñā* is usually translated as *recognition* or *recollection* and has been explained as the "knowledge" (*jñāna*) to which one "turns back" (*prati*), and which in turn "faces toward" (*abhi*) the knower. In this system recognition is the realization of the identity of the *jīvātman*, or individual self, with *paramātman*, the universal self. Pratyabhijñā is typified by the concept that the one reality is Śiva, and that Śiva expresses himself through Śakti with infinite *ābhāsas*, or manifestations. These manifestations are categorized as thirty-six *tattva*s, or constituents of the universe (compare with the twenty-five *tattva*s of Sāṃkhya); since they are the essence of Śiva, the *tattva*s are no less real than the five *kañcuka*s ("coverings") and the three *mala*s ("impurities") that constitute *māyā*, which causes the sense that one does not belong to the universal essence of Śiva, but instead has a separate identity.

The world of *saṃsāra* is a product of the limitations of *māyā*. These limitations cause the individual to remain bound, with a restricted viewpoint regarding his identity and capacities; this restriction causes him to forget his true nature. Pratyabhijñā teaches therefore that in order to overcome this false viewpoint, one must recognize that *saṃsāra* is not a separate reality, but is a manifestation of Śiva. When the individual acquires the recognition that Śiva not only enjoys *svātantrya*, or freedom, but exists also in everything that is limited and bound, he immediately recognizes that he, in turn, is identified with that which is unlimited and absolutely free.

Recognition implies that on every level, in every aspect of perception and of existence, the individual must recognize his unity with Śiva. If the universe is said to undergo a particular process, this process is necessarily recognized as one that may be experienced by the individual. If Śiva is said to constitute the whole universe, so, then, does the individual. In the explanation of how this operates, the texts emphasize the innate unity of the elements in the universe, and it will be seen that the same terms are applied to the processes of both the ultimate self and the individual one.

It is the nature of Śiva to become immanent and then to disappear continually, and this is done by means of his *śakti*, or power, personified as Śakti, who expands outward and then withdraws again. The *tattva*s, like Śiva himself, are said to be in a constant process of *sṛṣṭi* (creation) and *pralaya* (dissolution). This is also known as *unmeṣa* ("opening out") and *nimeṣa* ("closing down"). When Śiva "opens out" and becomes manifest, he is said to become bound and limited. It is thus in this state that the person of ordinary worldly consciousness remains bound in the world. But by identifying with higher and higher manifestations of Śiva, one can come to recognize the supreme state of Śiva—beyond manifestation—that is the body of consciousness itself. Thus does the bonded person become liberated, enjoying the freedom (*svātantrya*) of following the path of Śiva.

Pratyabhijñā provides a system by which one can work toward *samāveśa*, or immersion, and thus reintegration, by changing his sense of identity from that of the *paśu*, limited or bonded perceiver, to the *pati*, master of all processes. The system recognizes four graded *upāya*s (means, ways, paths); by traveling along these "paths" of Śiva, the aspirant learns to recognize that the "five functions" (*pañcakṛtya*s) of Śiva are functions that operate within himself as well. These eternal functions are *sṛṣṭi* (creation or emanation), *sthiti* (maintenance), *saṃhāra* (reabsorption), *vilaya* or *tirodhāna* (concealment), and *anugraha* (grace). The fifth, *anugraha*, is essential for the process of reintegration. It becomes manifest as the aspirant's devotion (*bhakti*) to the Lord. Thus in the songs of the *Śivastotrāvalī* devotion and grace are equally important. When the aspirant begins to effect the merging of his identity, he will recognize that the very act of his offering of devotion is but another aspect of the Lord's offering of grace.

Utpaladeva acknowledges that there is an array of systems claiming to lead to that goal of identifying with the ultimate. But the only one that he considers truly efficacious is the path of devotion. In the songs of the *Śivastotrāvalī* we follow the devotee Utpala on this path. These songs shed light not only on what a spiritual quest entails in theory—but they record the experiences and reflections of one as he travels along this arduous yet joyful journey.

Appendix B

The Manuscripts and their Variant Readings

A description of the manuscripts and printed edition examined in my original study of the *Śivastotrāvalī* is as follows.

B-1 = Banaras Hindu University Library, Catalogue No. 822 (No. 44); title: *Utpala Stotrāvalī*; script: *śāradā*; good condition; 17 × 12 cm; 1-20 of 72 folios; 27-50 lines of script; verses written slightly larger than commentary and are set apart for clarity.

B-2 = Banaras Hindu University Library, Catalogue No. 882 (No. 17/8259); title: *Utpalastotrāwalī*; script: *śāradā*; excellent condition; 12 × 10 cm; 1-57 of 121 folios; 16 lines of script; verses and commentary run together.

B-3 = Banaras Hindu University Library, No. 882 (No. 104); title: *Utpalastotrāwalī*; script: *śāradā*; good condition; 13 × 9 cm; 1-98 of 228 folios; 12 lines of script; verses and commentary run together.

J = Śrī Ranbir Sanskrit Research Library, Raghunāth Mandir, Jammu, Catalogue No. 1088; title: *Stotrāvalī Vivritti Advayastuti*; script: *devanāgarī*; good condition; 12.5 × 17.5 cm; 1-36 of 84 folios; 13 lines of script; verses and commentary run together.

K-1 = University of Kashmir Manuscript Library, Srinagar, No. 215; title: *Śivastotrāvalī*; script: *śāradā*; good condition; 24 × 19 cm; bound into book form; 20 lines of script; verses and commentary run together.

Appendix B

K-2 = University of Kashmir Manuscript Library, No. 1329.01; title: *Śivastotrāvalī*; script: *śāradā*; good condition; 19 × 13.5 cm; 1-39 of 80 folios; 10 lines of script; does not contain Kṣemarāja's commentary, but has another, brief gloss of certain words and phrases in margin and in between lines; elaborately decorated, painted border; includes two paintings in excellent condition.

P = Bhandarkar Oriental Research Institute, Pune, No. 507/1875-76; title: *Stotrāvalī with Vṛtti*; script: *devanāgarī*; excellent condition; 34 × 15 cm; 1-50 of 99 folios; 13-15 lines of script; verses written slightly larger than commentary and are set apart for clarity.

(C) = Chowkhamba Sanskrit Series printed text of *Śivastotrāvalī: The Śivastotrāvalī of Utpaladevāchārya*, ed. by Rājānaka Lakṣmaṇa, Chowkhamba Sanskrit Series, No. 15 (Varanasi: Chowkhamba Sanskrit Series Office, 1964).

The most common variants in the texts involved nothing more major than differences of *saṃdhi* and the insertion of synonyms, as in *svarūpa* for *śarīra* (4.25), *jagatām* for *lokānām* (10.1), and *visṛto* or *galito* for *prasṛto* (4.14). Common also is the interchanging of *vibho, prabho,* and sometimes *nātha* in the vocative. But these differences are slight, and the tradition of the text, as far as I have seen, is intact and contains no significant variants.

All of the manuscripts used for this study are on coarsely-grained paper indigenous to India, commonly referred to as "country paper;" all are written in black ink. K-2 is the only manuscript not in folio form; it has instead been bound into book form.

None of the manuscripts is dated, but K-2 may well be the oldest among them; though it is undated, it is considered by the pandits at the University of Kashmir manuscript library to be "250-300 years old." The conjecture is based on the feel of the paper and the beautiful and particularized style of the script. The scribe is thought to have been Rājānaka Ratnakaṇṭha, a well-known Kashmiri scribe whose signature appears on a dated manuscript of the *Rājataraṅgiṇī*.[1]

B-1, B-2, B-3, K-1, and K-2 are in *śāradā* script, and J and P are in *devanāgarī*. In deciphering the *śāradā* character I found the published materials on the script generally helpful only in the presentation of initial consonants and some vowels; certain other vowels, as well as compound consonants, are not represented adequately in script charts.[2] None of the works consulted notes, for instance, that when *ṇa* becomes *ṇā*, it is written with an entirely different *akṣara*, or that the *repha* does not appear above the letter it precedes, but is joined to the left of it, sometimes almost invisibly so.

Part of the difficulty with *śāradā* is that each scribe has his own style, and what is published in one chart may vary enough from the manuscript under study to cause considerable confusion; I have found such variations even within a single manuscript. In addition, *śāradā* causes particular problems for one accustomed to reading *devanāgarī*; certain of the *akṣaras* are "false friends," i.e., the *śāradā ṇa* is almost identical to the *devanāgarī la*, and its *tha* resembles the *devanāgarī ṣa*. The symbols for *ma, śa, sa,* and *a* not only resemble each other, but can be mistaken for the *devanāgarī bha* as well. The *śāradā bha*, however, is completely different from any character found in *devanāgarī*.

Manuscripts J and P are written in *devanāgarī*, and seem most likely to have had Kashmiri scribes. This is especially true of J, where not only does the formation of the characters resemble the angular style of *śāradā*, but in a few instances a *śāradā akṣara* is carelessly substituted for a *devanāgarī* one.

Certain scribal errors and variations common to both the *śāradā* and *devanāgarī* manuscripts have been left unrecorded in the footnotes to the text since they not only detract from the more significant variant readings, but they follow patterns that can be recorded here.

I have found these to fall into three categories: 1) omissions, 2) the interchange of one *akṣara* for another, and 3) *saṃdhi* errors and variant spellings.

Omissions in most cases are due to scribal carelessness. The interchanging of *akṣara*s can be attributed to the scribe's hearing a Sanskrit sound as it has become changed through the modern vernacular. Thus some of these permutations occur in manuscripts originating in an area where the vernacular has a Sanskrit base; others will be peculiar to manuscripts copied by Kashmiri scribes. It should be noted that in most cases the variations are of mutual interchange, that is, x does not exclusively replace y, but rather x is written for y in some places, and in others, y is written for x. The errors and variant usages of *saṃdhi* can be attributed both to carelessness of pen as well as an ear not well attuned to the sound of classical Sanskrit. Examples may be seen in the following:

1) omission of:
   - final *visarga.*
   - internal vowel, i.e., the additional stroke(s) required for *a, i, e,* etc.
   - *avagraha.* (In some manuscripts this is omitted consistently throughout the text.)
2) interchanging of:
   - *ra* and *ṛ.*
   - *va* and *ba.*
   - *na* and *la.*
   - *kha* and *kṣa.* (The interchange of these two sounds is so common in Kashmir that I have seen, in English, Kṣemarāja referred to as Khemarāja.)
   - modern vernacular *ḍa,* which places a *bindu* beneath the *akṣara,* used for Sanskrit *ḍa.*
   - all sibilants, especially *śa* and *ṣa.*
   - *va* and *u,* when following a consonant, i.e., *bhavjjvaṣāṃ* for *bhavajjuṣāṃ.* Another example also indicates misuse of sibilant: *haryaṣuviriñca* for *haryaśvaviriñca.*
   - nasal *akṣara*s and *anusvāra;* often without specific pattern, i.e., in one place *paṃka,* and another, *paṅka,* within one manuscript. The exception is in J, which uses *anusvāra* almost exclusively.
   - one nasal for another, i.e., *parāñmukho* for *parāṅmukho.*
   - *mṃ* for final *m* or *ṃ.*
   - aspirates and non-aspirates. The tendency is to de-aspirate, but interchanges occur both ways; i.e., *śambu* for *śambhu, ānandha* for *ānanda.* The most common occurrence is in the retroflex *varga;* i.e., *dṛṣṭhi* for *dṛṣṭi, abhīṣṭham* for *abhīṣṭam, tiṣṭasi* for *tiṣṭhasi.*
3) *saṃdhi* errors and variant spellings:
   - most common with *visarga saṃdhi;* i.e., *nāmagrahaḥ tasmai* for *nāmagrahas tasmai; jaladheḥ yutāḥ* for *jaladheścyutāḥ.*
   - final nasals; i.e., *bhraman asti* for *bhramannasti.*
   - final dentals; i.e., *madhyātbhavan* for *madhyādbhavan.*

Notes

INTRODUCTION

1. For elaboration of the Pratyabhijñā doctrine, see Appendix A.

2. Constantina Eleni Rhodes, *The Śivastotrāvalī of Utpaladeva: Sanskrit Devotional Poetry of Kashmir*, Columbia University, New York, 1983.

3. *The Śivastotrāvalī of Utpaladevāchārya*, edited by Rājānaka Lakṣmaṇa (Varanasi: Chowkhamba Sanskrit Series Office, 1964; Chowkhamba Sanskrit Series, No. 15).

4. For further details of my findings, see Appendix B.

5. See, for example, R. K. Kaw, *Doctrine of Recognition* (Hoshiarpur, 1967), pp. 360-361; Swami Muktananda, *Secret of the Siddhas* (Ganeshpuri, 1980), pp. 1-8; B. N. Pandit, *Aspects of Kashmir Śaivism* (Srinagar, 1977), pp. 40-45; and J. Rudrappa, *Kashmir Śaivism* (Mysore, 1969), p. xiii.

6. Pramathanath Mukhopadhyaya, "Tantra as a Way of Realization," *Cultural Heritage of India*, in 3 vols. (Belur Math, Calcutta: Sri Ramakrishna Centenary Committee, 1936), II, 172.

7. Vasudeva S. Agrawala, *Śiva Mahādeva: The Great God* (Varanasi: Veda Academy, 1966), pp. 4-7, 56-57.

8. Arabinda Basu, "Kashmir Śaivism" in *Cultural Heritage of India*. Edited by Haridas Bhattacharyya, 2d. rev. ed. in 5 vols. (Calcutta: Ramakrishna Mission Institute of Culture, 1956) IV, 85.

9. Harvey P. Alper, "Śiva and the Ubiquity of Consciousness," *Journal of Indian Philosophy* 7 (1979), p. 385.

10. *Śivadṛṣti*, cited in (and translated by) J. Rudrappa, *Kashmir Śaivism*, p. 97.

11. *Anubhāva Sūtra*, cited in (and translated by) J. Rudrappa, *Kashmir Śaivism*, p. 69.

12. Mariasusai Dhavamony, *Classical Hinduism* (Rome: Università Gregoriana Editrice, 1982), p. 228.

13. *Ibid.*

14. santyeva sūktisaritaḥ paritaḥ sahasrāḥ
     stotrāvalī surasarit sadṛśī na kācit /

Notes

yā karṇatīrthamastiśayya punāti puṃsaḥ
śrīkaṇṭhanāthanagarīmupakaṇṭhayantī //
Śāstra-parāmarśa of Madhurāja-yogin, verse 8 (available only in manuscript form), cited in Kanti Chandra Pandey, *Abhinavagupta: An Historical and Philosophical Study* (Varanasi: Chowkhamba Sanskrit Series Office, 1963; Chowkhamba Sanskrit Studies, No. 1, 2nd ed.), p. 765. The translation is my own.

Appendix A

1. R. K. Kaw, *The Doctrine of Recognition* (*Pratyabhijñā Philosophy*). (Hoshiarpur, Vishveshvaranand Institute, 1967; Vishveshvaranand Indological Series, No. 40), pp. 49-60.

Appendix B

1. Pandit Dina Nath Shastri, discussion at University of Kashmir, Srinagar, May, 1982.

2. Cf. Georg Bühler, *Indian Paleography* (Calcutta: Indian Studies: Past and Present, 1959; reprint); B. Ch. Chhabra, *Antiquities of Chamba State*, Part II: *Mediaeval and Later Inscriptions*, Archeological Survey of India, No. 72 (Delhi: Manager of Publications, 1957); Jayalal Kaul, *Studies in Kashmiri* (Srinagar: Kapoor Brothers, 1968); *Linguistic Survey of India*, Vol. VIII, Part II, ed. by G. A. Grierson (Delhi: Motilal Banarsidass, 1968; reprint of first edition, 1919); Louis Renou and Jean Filliozat, *L'Inde Classique: Manuel des Etudes Indiennes*, Bibliothèque De L'Ecole Française D'Extrème-Orient, Vol. III (Paris: Imprimerie Nationale, 1953).

Bibliography

I. PHILOSOPHICAL WORKS IN SANSKRIT

(Because of the variety of transliteration systems used by editors, the Sanskrit bibliographic entries will follow English alphabetical order.)

Gurunātha-Parāmarśa. Of Madhurāja. Edited by P. N. Pushp, Kashmir Series of Texts and Studies, No. 85. Srinagar: Research Department, 1960.

Īśwarapratyabhijñā of Utpaladeva. With the Vimarśinī of Abhinavagupta. In 2 vols., Kashmir Series of Texts and Studies, Nos. XXII, XXXIII. Vol. I (inaccurately) entitled: *Īśvara-pratyabhijñā Vimarśinī of Utpaladeva. With Commentary by Abhinava-Gupta.* Edited by Mukund Rām Shāstrī, 1918; Vol. II: Edited by Paṇḍit Madhusūdan Kaul Shāstrī, 1921. Śrīnagar: Research Department.

Īśvarapratyabhijñā Vivritivimarśinī by Abhinavagupta. Vols. I, II, III. Edited by Paṇḍit Madhusūdan Kaul Shāstrī, Kashmir Series of Texts and Studies, Nos. LX, LXII, LXV. Śrīnagar: Research Department, 1938, 1941, 1943.

Mahārtha-Mañjarī of Maheshvara Nanda. With Commentary of the Author. Edited by Mahāmahopādhyāya Paṇḍit Mukunda Rāma Shāstrī, Kashmir Series of Texts and Studies, No. XI. Śrīnagar: Research Department, 1918.

Mahārthamañjari. With the Commentary Parimala. Of Maheśvarānanda. Edited by Mahāmahopādhyāya T. Ganapati Śāstrī, Trivandrum Sanskrit Series, No. LXVI. Trivandrum: Superintendent, Government Press, 1919.

Mālinivijayottara Tantram. Edited by Paṇḍit Madhusūdan Kaul, Shāstrī, Kashmir Series of Texts and Studies, No. XXXVII. Śrīnagar: Research Department, 1922.

Bibliography

Parātrishika-Laghuvritti by Abhinavagupta. Edited by Paṇḍit Jagaddhara Zādoo Shāstrī, Kashmir Series of Texts and Studies, No. LXVIII. Śrīnagar: Research Department, 1947.

Parātrisika Vivriti of Rājānaka Lakshmirāma. Edited by Paṇḍit Jagaddhara Zādu Shāstrī, Kashmir Series of Texts and Studies, No. LXIX. Śrīnagar: Research Department, 1947.

Parā-trimshikā. With Commentary. The Latter by Abhinavagupta. Edited by Mahāmahopādhyāya Paṇḍit Mukunda Rāma Shāstrī, Kashmir Series of Texts and Studies, No. XVIII. Śrīnagar: Research Department, 1918.

Pratyabhijñā-kārikā-vritti. Of Rājānaka Utpala Deva. Edited by Paṇḍit Madhusūdan Kaul Shāstrī, Kashmir Series of Texts and Studies, No. XXXIV. Śrīnagar: Research Department, 1921.

Sarva-darśana-saṃgraha of Sāyaṇa-Mādhava. Edited by Mahāmahopādhyāya Vasudev Shāstrī Abhyankar, Government Oriental Series Class A, No. 4, 2nd ed. Poona: Bhandarkar Oriental Research Institute, 1951.

Shiva Sūtra Vārttika. By Bhaskara. Edited by Jagadīsha Chandra Chatterji, Kashmir Series of Texts and Studies, No. IV. Śrīnagar: Research Department, 1916.

Shivasūtra-Vārtikam by Varadarāja. Edited by Paṇḍit Madhusūdan Kaul, Shāstrī, Kashmir Series of Texts and Studies, No. XLIII. Śrīnagar: Research Department, 1925.

Shiva Sūtra Vimarshinī. Being The Sūtras of Vasu Gupta with the Commentary Called Vimarshinī by Kṣemarāja. Edited by J. C. Chatterji, Kashmir Series of Texts and Studies, No. I. Śrīnagar: Research Department, 1911.

Siddhitrayi of Rājānaka Utpala Deva. Edited by Paṇḍit Madhusūdan Kaul Shāstrī, Kashmir Series of Texts and Studies, No. XXXIV. Śrīnagar: Research Department, 1921.

Śivadṛṣṭi of Śrīsomanāndanātha. With the Vṛitti by Utpaladeva. Edited by Paṇḍit Madhusūdan Kaul Shāstrī, Kashmir Series of Texts and Studies, No. LIV. Śrīnagar: Research Department, 1934.

Spanda Karikas. With the Vivriti of Ramakantha. Edited by J. C. Chatterji, Kashmir Series of Texts and Studies, No. VI. Srinagar: Research Department, 1913.

Spanda Kārikās. With the Vṛitti by Kallaṭa. Edited by J. C. Chatterji, Kashmir Series of Texts and Studies, No. V. Śrīnagar: Research Department, 1916.

Spandakārikās of Vasugupta. With the Nirṇaya by Kṣemarāja. Edited and translated by Paṇḍit Madhusūdan Kaul, Shāstrī, Kashmir Series of Texts and Studies, No. XLII. Śrīnagar: Research Department, 1925.

Stava-Chintāmaṇi of Bhaṭṭa Nārāyaṇa. With Commentary by Kṣemarāja. Edited by Mahāmahopādhyāya Paṇḍit Mukunda Rāma Shāstrī, Kashmir Series of Texts and Studies, No. X. Śrīnagar: Research Department, 1918.

Tantrāloka of Abhinava Gupta. With Commentary by Rājānaka Jayaratha. In 13 vols., Kashmir Series of Texts and Studies. Śrīnagar: Research Department. Vol. I: Edited by Mahāmahopādhyāya Paṇḍit Mukund Rām Shastri, No. XXIII, 1918; Vol. XII: Edited by Paṇḍit Mukunda Kaul Shāstrī, No. LVIII, 1937.

II. STOTRA COLLECTIONS IN SANSKRIT

Bauddhastotrasaṃgraha, Or A Collection of Buddhist Hymns. Edited by Baron von Stael-Holstein, Bibliotheca Indica, Calcutta: Asiatic Society of Bengal, 1908.

Bṛhat Stotra Ratnākaraḥ. Varanasi: Thakur Prasad and Sons Booksellers, *saṃvat* 2035.

Brihat Stotra Sāgara. Bombay: Gujarati News Press, 1927.

Brihat Stotra Sarit Ratnākara. Bombay: Native Opinion Press, 1918.

Śivastotrāvalī of Utpaladevāchārya. With the Sanskrit Commentary of Kṣemarāja. Edited with Hindi commentary by Rājānaka Lakṣmaṇa, Chowkhamba Sanskrit Series, No. 15. Varanasi: Chowkhamba Sanskrit Series Office, 1964.

Stotraratnasaṃgraha. Mathura: Gita Press, no date given.

Stotraratnāvalī. Gorakhpur: Gita Press, no date given.

Stotrārṇavaḥ. Edited by T. Chandrasekharan, Oriental Manuscripts Series, No. 70. Madras: Government of Madras, 1961.

Bibliography

Stotrasamāhāra, Part I. Edited by K. Raghavan Pillai, University of Kerala Sanskrit Series, No. 211. Trivandrum: S. V. G. Press, 1964.

III. PHILOSOPHICAL WORKS IN TRANSLATION

Chakraborti, Haripada, trans. *Pāśupata Sūtram, with Pañcahārtha-Bhāṣya of Kauṇḍinya.* Calcutta: Academic Publishers, 1970.

Cowell, E. B., and A. E. Gough, trans. *The Sarva-darśana-saṃgraha or Review of the Different Systems of Hindu Philosophy of Mādhava Āchārya.* 2nd ed. London: Kegan Paul, Trench, Trübner and Co., 1894.

Gnoli, Raniero. *The Aesthetic Experience According to Abhinavagupta.* Serie Orientale Roma XI. Rome: Istituto italiano per il medio ed estremo oriente, 1956.

————, trans. "*Śivadṛṣṭi* by Somānanda," *East and West,* VIII, No. 1 (April, 1957), 16-22.

Kaw, R. K., ed. and trans. *Pratyabhijñā Kārikā of Utpaladeva.* Shārada Peetha Research Series, No. 12. Śrīnagar: Shārada Peetha Research Centre, 1975.

Lessing, Ferdinand D. and Alex Wayman, ed. and trans. *Mkhas Grub Rje's Fundamentals of the Buddhist Tantras.* Indo-Iranian Monographs, Vol. VIII. The Hague: Mouton, 1968.

Secret of Recognition (Pratyabhijñāhṛdayam). Edited by The Staff of the Adyar Library. German translation by Emil Baer. Authorised translation into English by Kurt F. Leidecker. Adyar, Madras: Adyar Library, 1938.

Singh, Jaideva, trans. *Pratyabhijñāhṛdayam: The Secret of Self-recognition.* 3rd rev. ed. Delhi: Motilal Banarsidass, 1980.

————, trans. *Śiva Sūtras: The Yoga of Supreme Identity.* With a special note by Swami Muktananda. Delhi: Motilal Banarsidass, 1979.

————, trans. *Spanda Kārikās.* With a special note by Swami Muktananda. Delhi: Motilal Banarsidass, 1980.

————, trans. *Vijñānabhairava or Divine Consciousness.* Delhi: Motilal Banarsidass, 1979.

182

Taimni, I. K., trans. *The Secret of Self-Realization:* (*Pratyabhijñāhṛdayam*). Adyar, Madras: The Theosophical Publishing House, 1974.

Wayman, Alex. *Yoga of the Guhyasamājatantra: The Arcane Lore of Forty Verses.* Delhi: Motilal Banarsidass, 1977.

IV. HYMNS AND POETRY IN TRANSLATION

Anantakrishna Sastri, R., trans. *Śiva Sahasranāma Stotra.* Madras: V. Ramaswamy Sastrulu and Sons, 1955.

Avalon, Arthur and Saubhagyavardhanī, trans. *Ānandalaharī or Wave of Bliss.* Madras: Ganesh and Co., Ltd., 1953.

Avalon, Arthur and Ellen Avalon, trans. *Hymns to the Goddess.* Madras: Ganesh and Co., Ltd., 1952.

Avalon, Arthur, trans. *Śiva-mahimna-stava.* Madras: Ganesh and Co., Ltd., 1953.

Brown, W. Norman, trans. *The Mahimnastava: Or, Praise of Shiva's Greatness.* American Institute of Indian Studies Publication, No. 1. Poona: American Institute of Indian Studies, 1965.

Griffith, Ralph T. H., trans. *The Hymns of the Ṛgveda.* New rev. ed. Delhi: Motilal Banarsidass, 1973.

Kaul, Jayalal, trans. *Lal Ded.* New Delhi: Sahitya Akademi, 1973.

Kingsbury, F. and G. E. Phillips, trans. *Hymns of the Tamil Śaivite Saints.* Calcutta: Association Press, 1921.

Macnicol, Margaret, ed. *Poems by Indian Women.* Calcutta: Association Press (Y.M.C.A.), 1923.

Mahadevan, T. M. P., trans. *The Hymns of Śaṅkara.* Delhi: Motilal Banarsidass, 1980.

————, trans. *Śaṅkara's Hymn to Śiva* (*Śivānandalaharī*). Madras: Ganesh and Co. (Madras) Private Ltd., 1963.

Bibliography

Miller, Barbara Stoler, ed. and trans. *Love Song of the Dark Lord: Jayadeva's Gitagovinda.* New York: Columbia University Press, 1977.

―――――, ed. and trans. *Phantasies of a Love-Thief: The Caurapañcāśika Attributed to Bilhaṇa.* New York: Columbia University Press, 1971.

Nandimath, S. C., L. M. A. Menezes, and R. C. Hiremath, ed. and trans. *Śūnyasaṃpādane,* Vol. I. Dharwar: Karnatak University, 1965.

Popley, H. A., trans. *The Sacred Kural.* 2nd ed. Calcutta: Y.M.C.A. Publishing House, 1958.

Raghavan, V., ed. *Devotional Poets and Mystics.* 2 parts. New Delhi: Government of India Publications Division, 1978.

―――――, ed. *The Great Integrators: The Saint-Singers of India.* New Delhi: Government of India Publications Division, 1966.

―――――, ed. *The Indian Heritage: An Anthology of Sanskrit Literature.* Bangalore: Indian Institute of World Culture, 1958.

―――――, ed. *Prayers, Praises and Psalms.* Madras: Natesan and Sons, 1938.

Ramanujan, A. K., trans. *Speaking of Śiva.* Baltimore: Penguin Books, Inc., 1973.

Silburn, Lilian. *La Bhakti.* Publications de l'Institut de Civilisation Indienne, Fasc. 19, Série In-8me, Etudes sur Le Śivaïsme du Kashmir, Tome 1. Paris: Editions E. De Boccard, 1964.

―――――, trans. *Hymns de Abhinavagupta.* Institute de Civilisation Indienne, Fasc. 31. Paris: Editions E. De Boccard, 1970.

Singh, Kushwant, trans. *Hymns of Guru Nanak.* New Delhi: Sangam Books, 1969.

Singh, Trilochan, trans. *Sacred Writings of the Sikhs: (Granth Saheb).* London: George Allen and Unwin Ltd., 1960.

Subrahmanya Sastri, Pandit S. and T. R. Srinivasa Ayyangar, trans. *Saundarya-Lahari (The Ocean of Beauty) of Śrī Śaṃkara-Bhagavatpāda.* Adyar, Madras: The Theosophical Publishing House, 1965.

Subramanian, V. K., trans. *Śivānandalahari of Śaṅkarācārya.* Sultanpet, Palghat: Educational Supplies Depot, 1969.

Tambyah, T. Isaac. *Psalms of the Śaiva Saints.* London: Luzac and Co., 1925.

Temple, Sir Richard Carnac, trans. *The Word of Lallā the Prophetess: Being the Sayings of Lal Ded or Lal Diddi of Kashmir.* Cambridge: University Press, 1924.

Thompson, E. J. and A. M. Spencer, ed. *Bengali Religious Lyrics: Śākta.* Calcutta: Association Press (Y.M.C.A.), 1923.

Vimalananda, Swami, trans. *Sri Vishṇu Sahasranāma Stotra.* Tirupparaitturai: Sri Ramakrishna Tapovanam, 1978.

Vishṇu Sahasranāma: The Thousand Names of Vishṇu. Ganeshpuri (District Thana, Maharashtra): Shree Gurudev Ashram, 1976.

Yocum, Glenn E., trans. *Hymns to the Dancing Śiva: A Study of Maṇikka-vācakar's Tiruvācakam.* Columbia, Missouri: South Asia Books, 1982.

V.   SOURCES RELATING TO RELIGION, PHILOSOPHY, POETRY, AND HISTORY

Agrawala, Vasudeva S. *Śiva Mahādeva: The Great God.* Varanasi: Veda Academy, 1966.

Alper, Harvey P. "Śiva and the Ubiquity of Consciousness: The Spaciousness of an Artful Yogi. *Journal of Indian Philosophy* 7 (1979) 345-407.

Appaswamy, A. J. *The Theology of Hindu Bhakti.* Indian Theological Library, No. 5. Bangalore: Christian Literature Society Press, 1970.

Bamzai, P. N. K. *A History of Kashmir.* Delhi: Metropolitan Book Co., 1962.

Banerji, Sures Chandra. *Cultural Heritage of Kashmir: A Survey of Kashmir's Contribution to Sanskrit Literature.* Calcutta: Sanskrit Pustak Bhandar [1965].

Barnett, L. D. "Notes on the *Śaiva Siddhāntam*," *Le Muséon,* Nouvelle Série X (1909), 271-77.

Basu, Arabinda. "Kashmir Śaivism," *Cultural Heritage of India.* Edited by Haridas Bhattacharyya, 2nd rev. ed. in 5 vols. Calcutta: Ramakrishna Mission Institute of Culture, 1956, IV, 79-97.

Bibliography

Bhandarkar, R. G. *Vaishṇavism, Śaivism and Minor Religious Systems.* Strassburg: Grunriss, 1913.

Bhattacharyya, Krishnachandra, ed. *Studies in Philosophy*, Vol. I. Calcutta: Progressive Publishers, 1956.

Bhattacharyya, Narendra Nath. *History of the Śākta Religion.* Delhi: Munshiram Manoharlal, 1974.

Bhattacharyya, S. P. "Cornerstones of Rasa-Ideology and the Śaiva Darśana of Kashmir," All India Oriental Conference, *Proceedings*, Nagpur, 1945.

_____. "Indian Hymnology," *Cultural Heritage of India.* Edited by Haridas Bhattacharyya, 2nd rev. ed. in 5 vols. Calcutta: Ramakrishna Mission Institute of Culture, 1956, IV, 464-78.

_____. "The Stotra Literature of Old India," *Indian Historical Quarterly*, I, Part 2 (1925), 340-60.

_____. *Studies in Indian Poetics.* Delhi: Munshiram Manoharlal, 1964.

Bühler, Georg. "A Detailed Report on a Tour in Search of Sanskrit MSS. Made in Kasmir, Rajputana and Central India," *Journal of the Bombay Branch of the Royal Asiatic Society*, Extra No. 34a (1877), 1-90.

Chaitanya, Krishna. *A New History of Sanskrit Literature.* Bombay: Asia Publishing House, 1962.

_____. *Sanskrit Poetics.* Bombay: Asia Publishing House, 1965.

Chakravarti, P. C. *Doctrine of Sakti in Indian Literature.* Calcutta: General Printers and Publishers Ltd., 1940.

Chatterji, J. C. *Hindu Realism.* Delhi: Swastika Publications, first Indian reprint, 1975.

_____. *Kashmir Shaivaism.* Chandigarh: Galav Publications, reprint, 1981 (reprint of first edition, 1914).

_____. "The Trika Philosophy of Kashmir," *J & K Research* Biannual, I, No. 1 (May, 1976), 9-12.

Dasgupta, S. B. *Aspects of Indian Religious Thought.* Calcutta: A. Mukherjee and Co., Pvt. Ltd., 1957.

Bibliography

Dasgupta, Surendranath, *A History of Indian Philosophy*, Vol. V: *Southern Schools of Saivism*. Cambridge: University Press, 1955.

_____. *A History of Sanskrit Literature*, Vol. I: *Classical Period*. 2nd ed. Calcutta: University of Calcutta, 1962.

De, Sushil Kumar. *Aspects of Sanskrit Literature*. Calcutta: K. L. Mukhopadhyay, 1959.

_____. *History of Sanskrit Literature*. Calcutta: University of Calcutta, 1947.

_____. *History of Sanskrit Poetics*. In two vols. 2nd rev. ed. Calcutta: K. L. Mukhopadhyay, 1960.

Descriptive Analysis of the Kashmir Series of Texts & Studies. Kashmir Series of Texts and Studies, No. 80. Srinagar: Research Department, [1958].

Dhavamony, Mariasusai. *Classical Hinduism*. Rome: Università Gregoriana Editrice, 1982.

_____. *Love of God According to Śaiva Siddhānta: A Study in the Mysticism and Theology of Śaivism*. Oxford: Clarendon Press, 1971.

Dutt, Nalinaksha, ed. *Gilgit Manuscripts (Introduction)*. Srinagar: His Highness' Government, 1939.

Farquhar, J. N. *An Outline of the Religious Literature of India*. London: Oxford University Press, 1920.

Frazer, R. W. *A Literary History of India*. London: T. Fisher Unwin Ltd., 1898.

Ghosh, Atol Behari, "Spirit and Culture of the Tantras." *Cultural Heritage of India*. Belur Math, Calcutta: Sri Ramakrishna Centenary Committee, [1936], II, 165-89.

Gonda, J. *Viṣṇuism and Śivaism*. London: University of London, The Athlone Press, 1970.

Grierson, G. A. "Śaivism, Kashmir," *Encyclopedia of Religion and Ethics*. Edited by James Hastings. New York: Charles Scribner's Sons, 1921, XI, 91-96.

Jash, Pranabananda. *History of Śaivism*. Calcutta: Roy and Chaudhury, 1974.

187

Bibliography

Kak, Ram Chandra. *Ancient Monuments of Kashmir.* London: The India Society, 1933.

Kalhaṇa's Rājataraṅgiṇī. Translated by Ranjit Sītārām Paṇḍit. New Delhi: Sahitya Akademy, [1968].

Kalhaṇa's Rājataraṅgiṇī: A Chronicle of the Kings of Kaśmīr. Translated by M. A. Stein. 2 vols. Delhi: Motilal Banarsidass, reprint, 1979 (reprint of first edition, 1900).

Kane, Pandurang Vaman. *History of Dharmaśāstra,* Vol. IV. 2nd ed. Poona: Bhandarkar Oriental Research Institute, 1973.

Kaula, M. S., ed. *A Short Review of the Research Publications (Kashmir State).* Kashmir Series of Texts and Studies. Śrīnagar: Research Department, [1923].

Kaw, R. K. "Compendium of *Pratyabhijñā* Philosophy of Kashmir," *Jammu and Kashmir State Research Biannual,* I, No. II (Nov., 1976), 4-14.

_____. *The Doctrine of Recognition (Pratyabhijñā Philosophy).* Vishveshvaranand Indological Series, No. 40. Hoshiarpur: Vishveshvaranand Institute, 1967.

_____. *"Pratyabhijñā* & Its Twin Doctrines of *Ābhāsavāda* and *Svatantryavāda,"* J & K Research Biannual, I, No. I (May, 1976), i-iii.

Keith, Arthur Berriedale, *A History of Sanskrit Literature.* Oxford: Clarendon Press, 1928.

Khosla, Sarla. *History of Buddhism in Kashmir.* New Delhi: Sagar Publications, 1972.

Koul, Pandit Anand. *The Kashmiri Pandit.* Calcutta: Thacker, Spink & Co., [1924].

Kramrisch, Stella. *The Presence of Siva.* Princeton: Princeton University Press, 1981.

Krishnamachariar, K. *History of Classical Sanskrit Literature.* Madras: T. T. Devasthanam Press, 1937.

Kumar, Frederick L. *Philosophy of Śaivism.* New Delhi: Oxford and I. B. H. Publishing Co., 1980.

Kundu, Nundo Lall. *Non-dualism in Śaiva and Śākta Philosophy.* Calcutta: Sri Sri Bhairabi Jogeswari Math, [1964].

Lorenzen, David N. *The Kāpālikas and Kālāmukhas: Two Lost Śaivite Sects.* New Delhi: Thomson Press (India) Limited, 1972.

Macdonell, Arthur A. *A History of Sanskrit Literature.* 2nd Indian ed. Delhi: Motilal Banarsidass, 1971.

——————. "Hymns (Vedic)." *Encyclopedia of Religion and Ethics.* Edited by James Hastings. Edinburgh: T. and T. Clark, 1914, VII, 49-58.

Masson, J. L., and Patwardhan, M. V. *Aesthetic Rapture.* In 2 vols. Poona: Deccan College, 1970.

Mitra, Khagendranatha and Asutosh Bhattacharyya, "Diffusion of Socio-Religious Culture in North India," *Cultural History of India.* Edited by Haridas Bhattacharyya. 2nd rev. ed. in 5 vols. Calcutta: Ramakrishna Mission Institute of Culture, 1956, IV, 515-32.

Mudaliar, Rao Sahib N. Muragesa, "Śaiva Literature," *Cultural Heritage of India.* Edited by Haridas Bhattacharyya. 2nd rev. ed. in 5 vols. Calcutta: Ramakrishna Mission Institute of Culture, 1956, V, 89-106.

Mukhopadhyaya, Pramathanath, "Tantra as a Way of Realization," *Cultural Heritage of India.* Belur Math, Calcutta: Sri Ramakrishna Centenary Committee, [1936], II, 165-89.

Muktananda, Swami. *Introduction to Kashmir Shaivism.* Oakland, California: S.Y.D.A. Foundation, rev. ed., 1977.

——————. *Meditate.* Albany: State University of New York Press, 1980.

——————. *Secret of the Siddhas.* Ganeshpuri, Maharashtra: Gurudeva Siddha Peeth, 1980.

Nagarajan, K. S. *Contribution of Kashmir to Sanskrit Literature.* Bangalore: Soobiah and Sons, 1970.

Nallaswami Pillai, J. M. *Studies in Śaiva Siddhānta.* Madras: Meykandan Press, 1911.

Narayana Ayyar, C. V. *Origin and Early History of Śaivism in South India.* Madras University Historical Series, No. 6. Madras: University of Madras, 1936.

Bibliography

Nīlamata Purāṇa, The. Edited and Translated by Ved Kumari Ghai. 2.vols. Srinagar: J & K Academy of Art, Culture and Languages, 1973.

O'Flaherty, Wendy Doniger. *Śiva: The Erotic Ascetic.* Oxford: Oxford University Press, 1973.

Padoux, André. *Recherches sur la symbolique et l'énergie de la parole dans certains textes tantriques.* Publications de l'Institut de Civilisation Indienne, Fasc. 21. Paris: Éditions E. de Boccard, 1975.

Pandey, Kanti Chandra. *Abhinavagupta: An Historical and Philosophical Study.* Chowkhamba Sanskrit Studies, No. 1. 2nd ed. Varanasi: Chowkhamba Sanskrit Series Office, 1963.

Pandey, Sangam Lal. *Existence, Devotion and Freedom: The Philosophy of Ravidāsa.* Allahabad: Darshan Peeth, 1965.

Pandit, B. N. *Aspects of Kashmir Śaivism.* Śrīnagar: Utpal Publications, 1977.

_____. *Śrī Kāśmīra Śaiva Darśana.* (In Hindi). Jammu: Śrī Ranbir Kendriya Sanskrit Vidyāpītha, 1973.

Plott, John C. *A Philosophy of Devotion.* 1st Indian edition. Delhi: Motilal Banarsidass, 1974.

Raina, A. K. "Contribution of Kashmir to Sanskrit Literature: An Introductory Survey," *J & K Research Biannual,* I, No. I (May, 1976), 13-16.

Raghavan, V. "Indian Poetry." *Princeton Encyclopedia of Poetry and Poetics.* Edited by Alex Preminger. Princeton: Princeton University Press, 1965, 384-94.

_____. "Methods of Popular Religious Instruction in South India." *Cultural Heritage of India.* Edited by Haridas Bhattacharyya. 2nd rev. ed. in 5 vols. Calcutta: Ramakrishna Mission Institute of Culture, 1956, IV, 503-12.

_____. *The Number of Rasa-s.* 2nd rev. ed. Adyar, Madras: The Adyar Library and Research Centre, 1967.

Raja, C. Kunhan. *Survey of Sanskrit Literature.* Bombay: Bharatiya Vidya Bhavan, 1962.

Rastogi, Navijivan. *The Krama Tantricism of Kashmir,* Vol. I. Delhi: Motilal Banarsidass, 1979.

Ray, Sunil Chandra. *Early History and Culture of Kashmir.* 2nd rev. ed. New Delhi: Munshiram Manoharlal, 1970.

Renou, Louis and Jean Filliozat, *L'Inde Classique: Manuel des Etudes Indiennes.* Bibliotheque De L'Ecole Francaise D'Extreme-Orient, Vol. III. Paris: Imprimerie Nationale, 1953.

Rudrappa, J. *Kashmir Śaivism.* Mysore: Prasaranga, University of Mysore, 1969.

Sakharpekar, S. G. "Evolution of *Śaivāgamas.*" All India Oriental Conference, *Proceedings and Transactions,* Baroda, 1933.

Sastri, K. A. Nilakanta. "An Historical Sketch of Śaivism." *Cultural Heritage of India.* Edited by Haridas Bhattacharyya. 2nd rev. ed. in 5 vols. Calcutta: Ramakrishna Mission Institute of Culture, 1956, IV, 63-78.

Sharma, L. N. *Kashmir Śaivism.* Varanasi: Bharatiya Vidya Prakashan, 1972.

Siddhantashastree, R. K. *Śaivism through the Ages.* New Delhi: Munshiram Manoharlal, 1975.

Sinha, Jadunath. *Śākta Monism: The Cult of Śakti.* Calcutta: Sinha Publishing House Pvt. Ltd., 1966.

Sircar, D. C., ed. *The Śakti Cult and Tārā: Proceedings of the Seminar on the Origin of Śakti Cult and Tārā (April, 1965).* Calcutta: University of Calcutta, 1967.

Smith, Wilfred Cantwell. *Towards a World Theology.* Philadelphia: The Westminster Press, 1981.

Stein, M. A. "Memoir on Maps Illustrating the Ancient Geography of Kasmir." *Journal of the Royal Asiatic Society of Bengal,* New Series LXVIII, Part I, Extra No. 2 (1899), 1-232.

Sufi, Al-Hājj G. M. D. *Kashīr: A History of Kashmir,* Vol. I. Lahore: University of the Panjab, 1948.

Tattwananda, Swami. *The Vaiṣṇava Sects, The Śaiva Sects, Mother Worship.* Calcutta: Nirmalendu Bikash Sen Gupta, no date given.

Thirugnanasambandhan, Sri P. *The Concept of Bhakti.* Madras: University of Madras, [1970].

Bibliography

Walimbe, Y. S. *Abhinavagupta on Indian Aesthetics.* Ajanta's Series on Aesthetics, No. 2. Delhi: Ajanta Publications, 1980.

Wayman, Alex. "The Human Body as Microcosm in India, Greek Cosmology, and Sixteenth-Century Europe." *History of Religions,* Vol. 22, No. 2 (Nov., 1982), 172-90.

Wilson, H. H. *The Hindu History of Kashmir.* 1st Indian ed. Calcutta: Susil Gupta (India) Private Limited, 1960.

Winternitz, M. *A History of Indian Literature.* Translated by S. Ketkar. 2 vols. New York: Russell and Russell, 1927.

Woodroffe, Sir John [Arthur Avalon] *The World as Power.* 3rd ed. Madras: Ganesh and Co. (Madras) Private Ltd., 1966.

VI. SOURCES RELATING TO EPIGRAPHY AND TEXTUAL CRITICISM

Bhāratīya Prachīn Lipi-Mālā. (In Hindi). New Delhi: Munshiram Manoharlal, 1971.

Bower Manuscripts, The. Edited by A. F. Rudolf Hoernle. Archaeological Survey of India, New Imperial Series, Vol. XXII, in 2 parts, text and plates. Calcutta: Superintendent of Government Printing, 1893-1912.

Bühler, Georg. *Indian Paleography.* Calcutta: Indian Studies: Past and Present, reprint, 1959.

Chhabra, B. Ch., ed. *Antiquities of Chamba State,* Part II: *Mediaeval and Later Inscriptions.* Memoirs of the Archaeological Survey of India, No. 72. New Delhi: Manager of Publications, 1957.

Critical Study of Sacred Texts, The. Edited by Wendy Doniger O'Flaherty. Berkeley Religious Studies Series. Berkeley: Graduate Theological Union, 1979.

Grierson, George A. *A Manual of the Kashmiri Language,* Vol. I. Oxford: Clarendon Press, 1911.

Katre, S. M. *Introduction to Indian Textual Criticism.* Poona: Deccan College Post-graduate and Research Institute, 1954.

Kaul, Jayalal. *Studies in Kashmiri.* Śrīnagar: Kapoor Brothers, 1968.

Kaye, G. R., ed. *The Bakhshālī Manuscript.* Archaeological Survey of India, New Imperial Series, Vol. XLIII, parts I and II. Calcutta: Government of India, 1927.

Linguistic Survey of India, Vol. VII, Part II: *Indo-Aryan Family. North-Western Group.* Edited by G. A. Grierson. Delhi: Motilal Banarsidass, 1968 (reprint of first edition, 1919).

Macdonell, Arthur A. *A Sanskrit Grammar for Students.* Delhi: Motilal Banarsidass, second reprint, 1979 (1926).

Monier-Williams, Sir Monier. *A Sanskrit-English Dictionary.* Delhi: Motilal Banarsidass, reprint, 1979.

Raina, Krishna. *Hindi aur Kaśmīrī Nirguṇ Sant-Kāvya: Tultātmak Adhyayan.* (In Hindi). New Delhi: Śārada Prakāśan, 1979.

Sircar, D. C. *Indian Epigraphy.* Delhi: Motilal Banarsidass, 1965.

Wade, Reverend T. R. *A Grammar of the Kashmiri Language.* London: Society for Promoting Christian Knowledge, 1888.

Wayman, Alex. *Analysis of the Śrāvakabhūmi Manuscript.* Berkeley: University of California Press, 1961.

Index

Index

Made in the USA
Middletown, DE
28 December 2020